Peter Fishe Reed

Incidents of the War

The Romance and rRealities of Soldier Life

Peter Fishe Reed

Incidents of the War
The Romance and rRealities of Soldier Life

ISBN/EAN: 9783744692175

Printed in Europe, USA, Canada, Australia, Japan

Cover: Foto ©Thomas Meinert / pixelio.de

More available books at **www.hansebooks.com**

INCIDENTS

OF THE

WAR;

OR, THE

ROMANCE AND REALITIES

OF

SOLDIER LIFE.

P. FISHE REED.

Entered according to Act of Congress, in the year 1862, by

.ASHER & CO.,

In the Clerk's Office of the District Court for the District of Indiana.

PREFACE.

In all the annals of warfare there have been no battles more prolific of curious incident, and individual bravery and recklessness, than those of the present rebellion. Men of previously civil natures have become daring heroes, rushing into danger regardless of consequences, and defying, to their very mouth, the murderous machines that deal such terrible death upon them. A bursting shell, instead of terror, produces a joke; a bullet or a bayonet, more fun than fear.

Sparta, in her palmiest days of heroism, recorded no greater deeds of daring and devotion, no more magnificent exploits or cooler bravery than have been exhibited by the soldiery of both armies of America. The Saracens, who, infatuated with the reverence of the terrible Crescent, swept through the eastern world like a tornado, who went forth "conquering and to conquer," till even invulnerable Rome trembled before that ominous Crescent, and the battle cry of "Allah, Allah;" nor the Crusaders, whose sacred Cross, in after years, sent terror to the Mohammedan ranks, could have shown a greater or truer devotion to the emblem of their power, than have the soldiers of the North for the Stars and Stripes, that emblem their liberty.

Our soldiers are brave, shrewd and reckless without parallel, and their deeds, like the oral traditions of ancient days, will be preserved in the hearts of the people forever; and these instances of individual prowess and valor, that are seldom found in pages of more ponderous volumes, are ever the fire-side histories that tell the true character of a people. To this end is this volume presented to the public.

INCIDENTS OF SOLDIER LIFE.

THE VALOROUS FIFTY-SEVEN.

It having become necessary for General Burnside to be made acquainted with the force and condition of the rebels at Fredericksburg, and the surrounding country, he requested a reconnoissance to be made in that direction. In answer to this demand, General Sigel selected his body guard, commanded by Captain Dahlgren, with a portion of the 1st Indiana and the 3rd Ohio Cavalry. It was a perilous undertaking, for to pass a hundred horsemen through forty miles of the enemy's territory, cross a large and bridgeless river, and dash into a town, which, it was expected, the rebels occupied in force, was no delicate operation; but it was one which the boys hailed as a holiday excursion.

After leaving Gainesville they took a circuitous route, and rode till night, when, after resting a few hours, they pushed on towards the river, which they reached just at daybreak, and there, upon the opposite bank stood Fredericksburg. Here they met with a difficulty which had not been considered in the scheme. When the Union troops evacuated the place, six months before, they burned the bridge, and it had not been rebuilt. The tide was full; so with a good deal of chagrin, and more impatience, they were compelled to wait for the ebbing of the tide. Making the best of their disappointment, they secreted themselves in the woods, and held council. It was impossible for them to remain concealed, in their present position, till night should give them an opportunity to again move under the shelter of its darkness, and it was equally impossible for them to cross the river at flood-tide.

At last two of the Indianians volunteered to ride along the river side and reconnoitre. Without being discovered, they passed down the river till they were some distance below the town, where they saw a ferryman on the opposite bank, and representing themselves as rebel officers, they ordered him to row over. He immediately obeyed, but had no sooner got fairly landed than he discovered his mistake, for he was made a prisoner, and compelled, by the severest threats, to give the scouts such information as they desired, the most important of which was that the town contained about six hundred armed men, mostly dragoons.

When this news was reported to Captain Dahlgren his purpose was fixed, and he determined, much as the enemy's force exceeded his own, to push boldly into the town. Luckily for them they had not yet been discovered, and as soon as the tide was sufficiently low, he took fifty-seven Indianians—leaving the Ohioans on the northern bank—and crossed the river. Reaching the opposite shore, they started at a slow trot, hoping to take the town by surprise; but their movement had been discovered; the alarm was spreading, and the town was all astir.

> "And there was hurrying to and fro,
> And gathering tears, and tremblings of distress,
> And cheeks all pale, which but an hour ago,"

were flushed with the security vouchsafed by six hundred chivalrous Southrons. The enemy was already partly in the saddle, and bewildered groups of horsemen were in every street.

Captain Dahlgren saw the danger attending the experiment, but he was not to be intimidated. He determined to fall upon them like a thunderbolt, and by thus increasing the confusion, which he perceived, effect his purpose. As they neared the town, he spoke a few encouraging words to his men, and then they increased their trot into a quick gallop. Swifter and swifter still they fly, and, whisking through the air like so many John Gilpins, the gallant fifty-seven, with drawn sabres, cheers and shouts, darted into the town, and recklessly rushed down the main street. Here a squad of rebel horsemen were getting into line, but, one terrific screech, a volley of pistolry, and one grand flourish of sabres, and the terror stricken chivalry ingloriously fled.

Turning down a cross street, without abating their furious gallop, the Captain and his sturdy followers came upon another squad of rebel cavalry. These made a desperate resistance, and for a short time the dire confusion of battle reigned supreme. The trampling of hoofs, the clattering of scabbards, the sharp, ringing clink of the sabres and the gory gashes that followed, the pistol flash and rattle, the tumbling, struggling and groaning of the horse and rider, the screaming of the women and children, the cheering and hurrahing of the victors—a short, sharp, terrible contest, and the town was in the possession of the gallant Fifty-seven.

Once the rebels attempted to recover what they had lost; but
a repetition of northern valor scattered them, and effectually
drove them from the town.

The fruits of this strange victory were thirty-one prisoners, a
number of horses and accoutrements, sabres, arms, etc. Captain
Dahlgren held possession of the town for three hours, long
enough to convince the terrified inhabitants that they were not
to be injured, and then retired.

During this conflict the rebels lost twelve, while but one of the
Indianians fell. This one brave fellow fought desperately,
through the whole engagement, when, after it was over, seeing
a large rebel flag waving from a window, he secured it, and
wrapping it around his body, was returning to his company,
when a fatal shot was fired from a window by one of the citizens.
He was brought to the northern shore and buried by his sorrow-
ing companions, beneath the forest pines.

What a thrilling picture is this! The sweep like a whirlwind
—the shout—the rout—the victory! Victory, not for personal
glory, nor for ambition, but for a beloved country. The fabulous
fame of the Black Horse cavalry fades into insignificance at this
glorious achievement of these valorous fifty-seven sons of the
west. General Sigel was in ecstacies over this victory, and well
he might be, for no exploit of the war excels it, and it will go
down to history as one of the grandest on record.

MINGO, THE CONTRABAND.

Among the contrabands who were employed to work on the
famous canal, that was to effectually, and forever, cut off Vicks-
burgh from civilization and "the rest of mankind," was a middle-aged negro, by the name of Mingo. He had formerly belonged to a pious old rebel, who owned a plantation some miles
east of Vicksburg. Mingo, one day, having obtained leave of
absence, came up to camp to review Uncle Sam's grand army,
and grander canal. While he was looking wonders at the operation of the picks and shovels, he was accosted by one of the
guard:

"Well, Cuffee, what do you think of it?"

"Doesn't know, boss; couldn't tell what de debil massa Linkum do wid dis big ditch."

"It's to bury the niggers in," replied the guard gravely.

"All ob um?" inquired Mingo, dilating his eyes to their utmost.

"Yes," replied the guard, "every d—n nigger in the South is to be pitched in here, and covered up."

"What for dat?" said Mingo.

"Because the nigger is the cause of all this war, and as soon as they are all out of the way, the war is over."

Mingo showed his white teeth, and replied:

"Spec's I doesn't bliebe dat, boss. If de niggas all killed off, de massas still hate de Yankee. Dey fight um always, if dere ain't no niggas. Spec's I know what dis ditch for, sah."

"Well, what do you think, Sambo?" said the guard.

"Spec's massa Linkum can't get all his big boats by Vicksburg, an' he dig dis big ditch so he hab a river all to hisself. My names not Sambo, sah; Mingo."

"Good for you, nigger. Would you like to be free, Mingo?" said the guard.

"Spec's I would, boss, neber tried um," replied Mingo mournfully.

"Who's your master?"

"Dey calls him pious Purdy."

"Pious, is he?"

"Yes, sah, pious wid de white folks, but de berry debil mong de niggas, sah."

"How's that? Don't he give you plenty of work to do, and plenty of liquor and licking, and all such like?"

"Yes, boss, plenty ob work, sure, and two licks to one licker."

"Well, Lincoln's going to set all the niggers free, shortly. How would you like that?"

"Bress God! I likes dat."

"But you are free now, Mingo."

"How's dat, boss?" said the negro with a perplexed look, "you's joking, boss."

"No siree. That's so. Don't you know that as soon as you come into our lines you are free? We can't hold *slaves* in the United States army."

"Fore God, den, boss, I neber goes back to old pious Purdy, sure," exclaimed Mingo earnestly. There seemed to be a new light breaking in upon his mind. He grinned comically enough, yet there was a good deal of solemnity in the grin, for he seemed to consider it a very precarious affair, and deemed that liberty was not to be obtained without some peril. The guard saw the working of his mind, and asked him if he would not like to work for Lincoln.

"Yes, boss," answered Mingo fervently, "I works for anybody what keeps Massa Purdy away from me."

"Well," said the guard, authoritively, "jump into the ditch and go to work, and come around Saturday night and get your money. Pious Purdy can't get you here."

"Does you pay niggas to work, boss?" asked Mingo, with some credulity.

"Of course we do: go to work."

Mingo needed no second invitation. He could scarcely realize the transmutation from slavery to freedom; but his bosom swelled with the idea, vague though it was, of liberty, and he sprang to the work with an alaerity he had never shown before. Saturday night came, and he sought for the guard who had promised him the pay, but not finding him, he mentioned the case to an officer, who laughed at him, and told him niggers did not need money. They must first learn what to do with it; and also added that until then *liberty* ought to he sufficient pay. This was somewhat of a disappointment, but Mingo had treasured up the sweet word *liberty*, and valued it, as a precious morsel under his tongue, and the very word was sufficient to cancel, at least, one week's labor. So he toiled on till the canal was finished, and all hands were dismissed. He then felt sure of obtaining his pay; but he could find no one who could tell him where to apply. For several days he hung around the camp with the other contrabands, hoping to obtain, if not pay for the past, some employment for the future, even though he should get no other pay than liberty; but none offered him even this.

At last the negroes became quite troublesome about camp, and were driven across the lines. There was neither labor nor liberty for them any longer. This was a severe blow to the unlucky Mingo, for he realized that he was in imminent danger of being captured by his master, and again returned to that bondage from which he felt he had so luckily escaped. In his wanderings he again got within the Union lines, and coming across a picket, was charged upon so furiously that he fled back to camp. Here he was met with the kicks, cuffs and jeers of the soldiers, till he was glad to make his escape. Again he encountered a picket, and this time was driven past the lines into the territory of slavery.

"Fore God," he exclaimed, as the guard threatened to shoot him, "liberty no great tings no how. De slabe gets much work an' little vittels—free nigga gets nothing. I knows what I does; I goes back to Massa Purdy, and be slabe again. Massa Purdy gib um poor vittels; Massa Linkum none. I's not had nary bite dis yer four days. Debil take Linkum! I goes back to massa."

Accordingly, full of this philosophy, and empty of the staff of life, Mingo reported to his master, who ordered him some cornbread and fifty lashes, and then set him to work.

Pious Purdy was a vicious rebel, and consequently a party of Union cavalry, who happened that way, took him prisoner,

confiscated his property, and freed his slaves. The most of
them were in ecstacies over their freedom; but Mingo had
learned better. He feared the worst, and his fears were not
groundless—the worst came. After mature deliberation he determined to go farther north.

· After many days toilsome travel, during which he subsisted
on berries, he came to a point on the Mississippi, where he discovered a company of soldiers. Not doubting they were Union
men, he at once threw himself on their mercy. But it was a
fatal mistake. They were a band of guerrillas, who immediately
took possession of the chattel, and set him to work as cook.
This was a happy situation for the starving Mingo, for he feasted
luxuriously. He was not badly treated, and began to chuckle
at his good fortune.

At this time the President's famous Emancipation Proclama-
tion was issued. This caused some uneasiness among the guerrillas. They had been traveling southward, and were now in
the neighborhood of Corinth. There they met a slave dealer
from Louisiana, and Mingo was sold, and soon transferred beyond the confines of liberty, and resold to a planter near Thibadeaux. This master proved more cruel, even, than Pious Purdy,
and Mingo made up his mind that neither slavery nor freedom
was anything worth living for. But the vagaries of Fate are
past finding out. A company of skirmishers from New Orleans
came upon this planter, took him prisoner, captured his cotton
and negroes, and Mingo was again a freeman in the Crescent
City.

During the skirmish at Thibadeaux, for the slaves were compelled to fight, Mingo received a troublesome wound. While in
New Orleans he chanced to fall into the hands of a good-hearted
Vermonter, named Stone, a private in a Vermont regiment, who
took pity enough on the poor contraband to minister somewhat
to his needs, which so attached him to his benefactor that Mingo
adopted him as his master, and followed him through weal and
woe, whenever he was allowed to do so. For sometime, after
Mingo recovered, he would steal out from the camp in the night
time. and go to his new master, while he would be on guard
duty, and amuse him with the quaint story of his slave live; but
this being discovered, he was forbidden this privilege.

One day Stone was detailed as one of a squad to guard some
prisoners, who had been captured. Mingo, always eager to follow his master, in spite of danger, got an old musket, and followed in the rear. These prisoners were confined in an old,
isolated stone building, that had been used as a store house, and
it was now truly full of old barrels and other rubbish, and
among this rubbish were secreted a lot of loaded muskets. which
the prisoners finding, they concluded to fight their way out to

liberty. They were a desperate set of fellows, and had been a terror to the loyal neighborhoods which they had taken delight to devastate. They expected death, and would rather risk their lives with the guard, who had not a fourth their number, than with the more fearful military powers at headquarters. Accordingly, when night came the prisoners burst through the doors and windows, and rushed, yelling, upon the guard; but they were prepared for them, for Mingo, out of curiosity to hear what the prisoners might have to say, crept up to the building and hid himself in some brushes under one of the windows, and overhearing the plan, had informed his master. A terrible battle ensued, in which the contraband engaged with as much zeal as the best of them. He used his musket and bayonet to good advantage, being careful, always, to make his attack upon the rear of any rebel that might be turned towards him. Twice, however, during the melee, he saved his master's life, by throwing himself before him. The guard at last proved victorious, and, though part of the prisoners escaped, the rest were secured.

During this action Stone showed such intrepidity and daring, that he was promoted, but it did him little good, as he had received a wound which so disabled him that he was unfit for duty, and he subsequently received his discharge from the service, and returned home. Mingo could not bear to leave his master, and begged to follow him to his mountain home. Stone consented, and Mingo is now a free man in the maple clad hills of Vermont. But he sighs for his native land, and begs his master, that when the war is over, he will take him to work the cotton and the cane, in a climate that has no ice and snow.

STUMPY, THE SCOUT.

A soldier in the convalescent hospital at Louisville, related to the Surgeon the following bit of adventure:

Just before the battle of Corinth, I was detailed as one of a small scouting party. We brushed it about for some hours without seeing any thing worthy of note, and we began to think that we should have to venture farther into the enemy's lines, when, all of a sudden, our ears were saluted with the roar of a score or two of rebel carbines. It was a company of cavalry, numbering six to our one. One of our party was killed outright, which was all the damage done, and that counted a good deal with us, for he was a brave young fellow from Indiana, who was always in front when there was danger ahead. Poor George, he looked so brave and defiant, even as he lay there dead!

As soon as the rebels discharged their pieces they pounced upon us with their sabres, screaming like so many demons, but their yells did not intimidate us. We were used to such rebel music, and we joined in the chorus, and gave them back good base and treble for their wild tenor.

"Now, boys," sung out our Lieutenant, who was a joking sort of a fellow, and as brave as a beetle, "it is about dinner time. If you are hungry, just walk into them butternuts. Forward! and crack away!"

There was no time for further orders, nor did we need any. The rebels were coming down upon us like mad; but their carbines were empty, and ours were not. Each of us discharged his piece to the best advantage, and I'll venture to say that more than one horse and rider parted company. Sabres now became the order of the fight; and a terrible hand to hand fight it was, too. Our Lieutenant pitched upon a sturdy looking rebel, who was more than his match. The consequence was that our leader was wounded, and so disabled as to be unable to fight or give command. By this time we were entirely surrounded, and the most of us, I guess, began to think it was time, either to surrender or make a break.

At this moment, as good luck would have it, one of the rebels, coming up behind me, aimed a blow at my head. I saw it in season, and spurring my horse violently, he sprang forward just in time to save me; but this forward movement brought his tail out in a straight line, and, unluckily for the poor horse, the sabre came down upon his extended rear and cut it clean off close up to the rump. He kicked up once, and then bounded through the bristling sabres at a terrible rate, and took a bee line direct for camp, which was very satisfactory to me, as I had no control of him.

This movement of mine, though accidental, seemed to be the signal for the rest, and they made a like attempt to escape, but only one succeeded, who followed close at my heels. Some dozen or so of the rebels followed us, but our horses were the fleetest, and we gained on them. Before I had gone two miles I met a large company of our cavalry, who, having heard the firing, were coming to our aid. I managed to rein up my horse, and tell them the state of affairs, but had no sooner done so than the squad of rebel horsemen who had been pursuing us, came suddenly round a grove of brush, and, before they were aware of our presence, plunged headlong into our midst. Of course they were made prisoners, every one of them. I was detailed as one of the guard to take charge of them, and I had the satisfaction of taking into camp the very fellow who had amputated my horse's tail. The rest of the party then made hasty tracks for the rest of the rebel squad, which were soon found and captured, and the whole posse of them were safe at the rear of our camp.

The boys laughed at the odd appearance of my horse, and ever after called me "Stumpy." I did not feel very bad about it, for it was not the first engagement where the rebels have cut off our rear.

My horse was not much injured by his loss, and in a short time I was again out scouting. This time I was wounded and taken prisoner, and after lying in the rebel's starving camp for ten weeks, during which time I had a turn of the bilious fever, I was at last exchanged, and, although with an unhealed wound, and reduced to a mere shadow, I was marched, two hundred miles, into the Yankee nation.

It is a ticklish life the scout leads.

A NAMELESS PASS AND A NAMELESS GENERAL.

While the Union troops were stationed at Nashville, a citizen called at headquarters for a pass. The clerk wrote it all in proper order, and gave it to the General for his signature. There not being a table handy, the General placed the document up against the whitewashed wall, and wrote his name with a pencil. The citizen left with his pass, but was much astonished and dismayed when presenting it to the picket post, to find that his pass had no signature. He knew that he had seen the General write his name, and he could not imagine by what process of magic his signature had disappeared; but upon returning to headquarters the mystery was solved. His chagrin was changed to mirth, for there, upon the whitewashed wall, in suspiciously shaky looking letters, was the name and title of the signer. The joke was obvious. The General had probably been testing the strength of a certain contraband article, and in consequence of the obliquity of vision thereby occasioned, had written his name under the pass instead of upon it. In consequence of its being the General's first offence, the name is withheld.

Sadder results than this have resulted from a too free use of contraband brandy.

It may not be that this vice prevails to any great extent in the Union army, but one can not help thinking that more bullets and less brandy would be more effectual in subduing the enemy, unless the fiery liquid be distributed to the latter, for the same purpose as the bullets.

EAR-BREADTH ESCAPES.

A German in the 35th Illinois met with two very narrow escapes in fifteen minutes, while General Carr's division was contending so vigorously against the enemy in Cross-Timber Hollow. He wore ear-rings, for the benefit of his eyes, and a musket-ball cut one of them in two (the broken segments still remaining), and passed into the shoulder of the Second Lieutenant of the company.

"M▇▇ Gott!" exclaimed the brave Teuton, fingering the disse▇▇d ring.

Ten minutes later there was a lull in the battle storm, and the German was earnestly relating the story of his escape, when a wandering bullet whistled by, carrying the other ring with it, and abrading the skin of his ear, without doing further damage.

"Gott sei dank!" he said, fervently, "I got no ring in my nose!"

Such are the vagaries of fate; such the mysterious shiftings on the boisterous battle-field, in the great struggle of Life and Death!

A MISSOURI JIBBENAINOSY.

A member of the 9th Missouri discovered his brother horribly mangled and scalped. In his rage he swore vengeance against the Indians, and for the remainder of the day devoted his attention entirely to them, concealing himself behind trees and fighting them in their fashion. He was an excellent marksman, and if an Indian did but show him a square inch of his red skin, he was sure to send a bullet through it. Whenever an Indian dropped, in answer to the crack of the federal rifle, he would shout with delirious joy:

"There goes another red-skin to h——l. Hurrah for the Stars and Stripes, and d——n all the Indians!"

Though ever following the wily foe, and though fired upon again and again, he received not a scratch; and on his return to camp, after night-fall, bore with him nine scalps of aboriginal warriors, slain by his own hand to avenge his brother's death.

BULLET PROOF.

A forage wagon of the 36th Indiana, containing only the teamster and a private of company D, was attacked by a band of guerrillas. The discharge of a score or two of muskets tore the teamster into atoms, and relieved him of his command in a twinkling, while his comrade did not receive a scratch. Three of the rebels then advanced, on double quick, to within twenty feet of the Hoosier, two of them with double barreled shot guns, the other with a rifle, and, cowardly assassins as they were, fired upon the lone Yankee. But again "Fortune favored the brave." He was still unharmed, and sat there eyeing his coming captors as though he had not been the target upon which the chivalrous Southrons had been displaying their skill. The rebels, considering him bullet proof, refused to waste any more ammunition upon him, and took him prisoner.

It is but just to say that the bullet proof Hoosier was unarmed, or he would have shown the barbarous rebels a different marksmanship.

REBELS CAUGHT IN THEIR OWN TRAP.

The Sergeant of the picket guard being stationed near Pohick Church, had his attention drawn to the tinkling of a cow-bell in the bushes. With visions of new milk running through his head he examined carefully, and to his intense astonishment found himself euchered of his milk: but he made the discovery that, as he advanced, the cow-bell retreated. The Sergeant smelt a moderate sized mice, and made a double-quick retrograde movement. He immediately reported the affair to Colonel Hays. The Colonel secreted a squad of men in the woods, and the Sergeant again made himself conspicuous. He brushed about among the bushes, and the cow-bell approached. The squad soon had the satisfaction of seeing—not the cow, but a Secesher, with a cow-bell hung to his neck, and a six shooter in his belt. When he got within easy range, and in sight of the squad, the Sergeant hailed him:

"I say, old fellow, would you rather go to h—l or to Washington?"

The squad at the same time rushed forward.

"To Washington, I reckon," drawled the rebel, "I ain't clothed for a warm climate."

And he accordingly delivered himself up with the best possible grace.

A SAD RESULT OF THE WAR.

A Union man of Missouri, who had two brothers in the rebel army, joined the Home Guard, and a few days after one of his brothers rode up and found him practising with his rifle.

"I am glad to see you using your gun," said the brother. "You had better join a company."

"I have done so," was the calm reply.

"Is that so? What company is it?"

"The Home Guards."

"Ah, that's what you're at is it?" cried the brother. "Well here's something for you;" and he immediately drew a navy revolver and fired. The ball lodged in the breast of the other, who staggered and fell, but getting upon his knees and seizing his rifle, pointed it at his murderous brother, who turned and fled▮▮▮▮t there sped a sure ball from that trembling rifle, and it arrested the rebel brother's course forever.

LAST WORDS.

When General Reno was killed, General Sturgis was within a few yards of him. He was in command of the division formerly commanded by Reno, increased by several new regiments, and the men had just distinguished themselves in driving the rebels from the summit of the Blue Ridge. These General were bosom friends; had been classmates at West Point, and graduated together. When Reno fell, Sturgis ran to his assistance, had him picked up, and said:

"Jesse, are you badly hurt?"

"Yes, Sam," he replied, "I am a dead man."

"Great God, no!" exclaimed Sturgis.

"Yes, it is so, Sam, and you must do double duty now."

General Sturgis had him placed upon a litter and carried to the rear, where he died in an hour. His last words before leaving the battle-field. were: "Boys, I can be with you no longer in body, but I am with you in spirit."

Corporal Mooney, seeing that the staff of the regimental flag was shot away, picked up the Stars and Stripes, and wrapping them round his body, rushed over the parapet of the outworks, shouting gleefully: "Come on, me brave boys."

It was all he said. The next instant a shell struck him, and the flag and the Corporal were torn in pieces.

A soldier fell mortally wounded. Some of his comrades wished to carry him to the rear, but General Lew. Wallace riding by at the moment, ordered them to desist.

"We can not stop to attend to the wounded till the battle is over," said the General.

"You are right," replied the groaning soldier; "the country first. Boys go to your duty."

These were his last words. When the General again rode
that way, the devoted soldier's pains were over. He was dead.

The army was retreating from Centerville. The battle was
fought against a rebel force that had penetrated five miles
nearer Washington than our rear, and was moving to strike upon
the flank. General Stevens' division, the advance of Reno's
corps, was on the left of the road taken by the trains, and inter-
cepted by the enemy. He saw that the rebels must be beaten
back at once, or during the night they would stampede the wagons, and probably so disconcert our retreat that the last divisions
would fall a prey to their main force. He decided to attack
immediately, at the same time sending back for support. Having made his dispositions, he led the attack on foot at the head
of the 79th (Highlanders). Soon meeting a withering fire, and
the Color Sergeant, Sandy Campbell, a grizzled old Scotchman,
being wounded, they faltered. One of the color guard took up
the flag, when the General snatched it from him. The wounded
Highlander at his feet, cried:

"For God's sake, General, don't you take the colors; they'll
shoot you if you do!"

"Give me the colors!" demanded the officer. "If they don't
follow me now, they never will;" and he sprang forward with
the colors in his hand, crying:

"We are all Highlanders; follow brave Highlanders; forward
my Highlanders!"

The Highlanders did follow their Scottish chief, but while
sweeping forward a ball struck him on his right temple. He
died instantly. An hour afterward, when taken up, his hands
were still clenched around the flag-staff.

Thus ended the brave career of the brave Stevens. He had often
remarked that if it were his fate to fall in battle, he hoped he
should be shot through the temple and die instantly.

The day after the battle of Donelson, some of the rebel prisoners were permitted to go in search of their wounded. While
these prisoners were wandering through the woods, they came
upon the body of a dead soldier. One of the rebels gave it a
kick, at the same time saying:

"Take that, you yellow-bellied son of a ——."

"And that," said another voice near by; and a third voice,
also, uttered its quick, sharp, crack, and the impious, rebel
dropped dead with a bullet in his heart, and the filthy word still
groaning on his lips. The Union soldier who accompanied him
thus avenged the insulted dead.

The rebel General Ben. McCulloch was struck with a minie rifle
ball in the left breast, while waving his sword and encouraging

2

his men to stand firm. He died of his wounds about 11 o'clock the same night, though he insisted that he would recover; repeatedly saying with great oaths that he was not born to be killed by a d—d Yankee.

A few minutes before he expired his physician assured him he had but a very brief time to live. At this Ben. looked up incredulously, and saying, "Oh, Hell!" turned away his head, and never spoke after.

A REBEL SURGEON AND HIS SPUNKY UNION PATIENT.

At the bombardment of Fort Henry, a young Wisconsin boy, in his eagerness to "get a pop at a rebel," got detached from his company, and took a zigzag way towards the biggest crowd, firing as he went, and dodging, here and there, behind the circumstantial breastworks. Presently he found himself surrounded, and he had the honor of being made a prisoner of war. Not long after he had his arm shattered by a ball from one of the Union gunboats. He was taken to a tent, and the Surgeon commenced the work of amputation. He had just bared the bone, when a shell came crashing through the tent. The boy did not seem to pay much attention to the sawing of the bone, but coolly remarked:

"Them shells are staving things—don't they make you rebels get, though?"

Presently another shell shrieked and fell close by them.

"It is getting most too hot here for us, my boy," said the Surgeon. "I'll take you to a safer place."

"Too *hot* is it?" said the mangled boy. "Well, I guess it will be a good deal hotter for you by and by."

The Surgeon told the story with some pleasure, and remarked:

"He was the bravest little fellow I ever saw. I should like to meet with him again."

SHARP SHOOTING DUEL.

A rebel lieutenant was stationed in a rifle pit, and about fifty yards from him was a Berge sharp-shooter, well fortified by a huge tree. The Lieutenant could not lift a finger but the Berge gave him a pop. He had thus been the target for some time, when getting out of patience, he poked his head above the breastworks and shouted:

"Come out from behind that tree, you skulking Yankee."

"Come out from behind that breast work, you cowardly rebel, and see how you like it," was the prompt rejoinder.

The Lieutenant seized a musket, and springing over the works, sung out:

"Now, come on, you Nigger-stealer."

"Here's at you, you thieving Butternut," returned the Berge, stepping squarely from behind the tree, and in this position each took three fair shots at the other. Berge's third shot just lifted the hair from the other's ear.

"Go back to your tree," said the Lieutenant.

"Go back to your hole," returned the Berge, and both returned to their places of concealment.

Each, during the duel, was so eager to kill the other first, that both fired with bad aim. The Lieutenant was afterwards taken prisoner.

THE ESCAPE OF FLOYD AND PILLOW.

The official Rebel report of the decamping of Floyd and Pillow, and of the manner of the surrender of Fort Donelson, is as follows:

General Pillow urged the necessity of cutting their way out, or making another day's fight.

"From the worn out condition of my men,' replied Buckner, "and the enemy's rifle pits on the right, I cannot hold my position for half an hour, if we should be attacked at daylight, which will certainly be the case."

"Why can't you? I think you can sir," said Pillow. "I think, Sir, we ought to cut our way through at all hazards."

"I know my position," retorted Buckner. "I can only bring to bear against the enemy four thousand men, while he can oppose me with any given number."

"Well, gentlemen," said Pillow, "I am in favor of fighting it out. What will you do?"

"What do you say, General Buckner?" asked Floyd.

"Just this: that to attempt to cut our way through the enemy's lines, with such devils to fight with, will cost a sacrifice of three-fourths of the command, and no General has a right to make such a sacrifice to secure his own safety."

"I agree with the General on that point," said Floyd.

"Well," said Pillow, "there is but one alternative left, and that is capitulation. I shall neither surrender the command nor myself; I will die first."

"Neither will I surrender," retutned Floyd. "You know my

relations with the Federal Government, and it would not do. Their book of reckoning is already frightfully full."

"No personal feeling ought to control official action," said Buckner.

"I admit it," said Floyd. "Still my determination is fixed."

"The surrender will then devolve upon me," said Buckner.

"General Buckner," said Floyd, "if you are put in command, will you allow me to take out my brigade?"

"Yes," replied Buckner, "if you move your command before I send my offer of capitulation to the enemy."

"Then," said Floyd, "I surrender the command."

This declaration left the command upon General Buckner, and he replied:

"I will accept it, and will share the fate of my command," and he at once called for pen, ink and paper, and a bugler to sound a parley, it being too dark to send a flag of truce.

General Pillow then asked if it would be proper for him to make his escape. To which Floyd replied, that was a question for every man to decide for himself; but that he would be glad for every man to make his escape that could.

Colonel Forrest then desired to take out his command, which was granted.

"Now," said Forrest, "what shall I do?"

"Cut your way out," said Pillow.

"I will, General, by ——," said Forrest.

Among all the boasted chivalry massed at Fort Donelson, General Buckner was the only one who could stand the test of honor. True to his word, he followed his command and made himself a prisoner; while the officer in command, Floyd, to use his own words, sought "to make an effort for my own extrication by any and every means that might present themselves to me."

CAPTURE OF A FULL BLOOD.

During the grand retreat of the enemy across Roanoke Island, Captain Bradford, of a Massachusetts regiment, saw a man spring from a clump of bushes and run like a deer across an open space.

The Captain several times called to him to stop, but finding he was about to lose his game, ordered his men to fire. The rebel heard the order and immediately whirled around, and holding up both hands, cried;

"Don't shoot; *please* don't shoot!"

The order was countermanded, and the man tremblingly advanced and surrendered himself. He was a Quartermaster.

Not long afterwards, fifteen or twenty prisoners were drawn up around a good fire, and the "Special Artist" began making a sketch. This roused the chivalric pride of the rebel Quarter-master, who had by this time got over his fright, and approaching the artist, he said:

"I suppose you're some Yankee newspaper man and I want you to remember that, though I ain't as good looking as some o' the rest in this crowd, I've got jest the same kind o' Southern blood in my veins."

Somebody present remarked: "Perhaps that was the reason you whined so dolefully over in the field, yonder. You were afraid you'd lose some of that precious blood."

A SMART CHANCE.

When Commodore Goldsborough arrived at Croaton Sound, a fellow was presented to him who was recommended for a pilot, when the following conversation ensued:

Commodore.—"Well, sir, they say you know something about this Sound."

Pilot.—"Well, yes, mebbe four or five years ago I had a smart knowledge of that strip of water, Sir."

Com.—"How much water is there on this shoal?" (pointing to the chart.)

Pil.—"Well, I reckon there's a right smart chance of water there Sir."

Com.—"Did you pilot boats up and down the Sound?".

Pil.—"Well, yes; I reckon I've driv a few flat boats up thar, Sir."

Com.—"Can you give us any assistance by pointing out the safest way to get up there?"

Pil.—"Well, I reckon I could help you a right smart chance."

Com.—"Well then we want you."

Pil.—"But, your honor, I rather would'nt, Sir."

Com.—"What! don't you want to serve your country?"

Pil.—"Well, yes, but the old woman and young 'uns has got powerful little to live on, Sir."

Com.—"But we will pay you good wages."

Pil.—"And I hav'nt anything but these yeller old sou' westers, Sir."

Com.—"We'll give you good clothes."

Pil.—"B-b-but—"

Com.—"But what, Sir?"

Pil.—"Well, you see, your honor, you see that mebbe ef you

should'nt get up thar, them ar secessioners would use me powerful bad, Sir."

This devoted Union man was dismissed, with orders to hold
himself in readiness to lend a "right smart chance" of his aid to
the expedition.

TERRIBLE DEVOTION.

The sinking of the Cumberland was one of the most terrible
catastrophes of the war, and no instance shows a more desperate and devoted spirit than was shown by her brave crew. They
behaved with remarkable and stoical courage, continuing to
work every gun above the water line to the last moment, and
one of her guns was actually discharged at the enemy as she
was going down. There was no effort to escape, no rush to the
boats, not a sign of surrender, and every one of the three hundred brave sailors was buried beneath the water.

The terrible devotion of the crew of this ill-fated ship is
unparalleled in the annals of warfare.

As the ship was sinking, two gunners clasped their guns in
their arms and would not be removed. They went down em-
bracing them.

One gunner had both his legs shot away. Another shot had
torn him badly in the abdomen, and so, with his bowels protru-
ding, he made three steps on his raw and bloody thighs, seized
the lanyard and fired his gun, falling back dead.

Another lost both arms and legs, yet lived, and when they
would assist him, cried out:

"Back to your gun, boys! Give 'em hell! Hurrah for the
Flag!"

When asked to surrender the Cumberland, Lieutenant Morris
replied:

"Never! I will not strike my flag." Then, turning to his
men, he asked: "Would you do it?"

"No!" was the firm reply of all, and they did not do it.
When the ship was sinking the old flag still waved above her.

APPLE BRANDY.

When the Union soldiers entered the rebel fortifications at
Mill Spring, one of them discovered a barrel which proved to
contain apple brandy. Pulling out the corn cob from the bung

hole, he turned it up and filled his canteen. While d)ing this one of Bob McCook's skirmishers came in and said:

"Vat you gets dere?"

The soldier replied that it appeared to be pretty fair apple brandy; upon which the Dutchman ran to the door, calling out furiously:

"Hans! Heinirch! Schnapps! See here!"

Then rushed in a squad of his comrades, and the brandy was transferred to their canteens in a twinkling. The soldier was fond of a joke, and remarked seriously:

"Boys, this is a doctor's shop, and there *might* be strychnine in that brandy."

The thirsty Tuetons paused a moment, when one of them exclaimed:

"Py G—t! Hans, I tells you vat I does; I trinks some, and if it don't kills me, den you trinks mitout no danger."

He then took a long pull at his canteen, smacked his lips, and said:

"All·right, boys, go ahead."

THE TABLES TURNED.

When Fort Sumter surrendered, the following lines appeared in some of the Southern papers:

> "With mortar, Paixhan and petard,
> We tender to Old Abe our Beauregard."

Things having changed somewhat, and the rebels catching it front and rear, causing them to flee from the wrath to come, our Western friends now return the rebel's poetic courtesies in this wise:

> "With the rebels all routed and flying with fear,
> We tender Jeff. Davis our Foote in his rear."

KEEN PICKETS.

A soldier from Maine being on picket duty, was fired upon by one of the rebel pickets, from Georgia, the ball whizzing close to his ear. Upon this the Yankee sheltered himself behind a tree and began to look about for the concealed foe. Presently a little puff of smoke revealed the spot, and another ball paid its respects to his hair.

"Hello!" said Maine, "what are you trying to make?"

"Trying to wing a nigger stealer," said Georgia.

"Sho !" responded Maine, "I'm glad you told me. I should'nt have guessed it from your shootin'. Who made your old musket?"

"The London Times; who made your'n?" says Georgia, jumping behind his tree, while the Yankee's bullet sprinkled the bark in his face.

"Horace Greeley," said Maine.   "Where's Jackson?" ·

"Behind the wall," replied Georgia, at the same time barking the Yankee's tree.   "What's McClellan doing?"

"Reviewing the grand army."

"Got any whisky?" says Georgia.

"Only gunpowder, which you're welcome to," replied Maine, at the same time giving the rebel another pop.

"I say," says Georgia, "step out and give us a show."

The Yankee pokes out his head, and the rebel cracks away and misses.

"Too high, old feller. Now let me have a pop," said Maine.

Georgia pokes out his head and the ball passes between his chin and shoulder.

"Too low!" shouts the rebel.   "Let's quit a while and go home and practice."

"Quit it is," said Maine. 'Spose we adjourn for rations."

"Agreed," says the other.

And the two marched away, one whistling Dixie and the other Yankee Doodle.

REBELLION FINANCED DOWN.

Poor Beauregard for three month's soldiers prays,
    For which he bounty promises and thanks,
But Louisiana drafts at ninety days,
    Can't meet the checks on Mississippi banks.

CONTRABAND PHILOSOPHY.

An elderly darkey, with a very philosophical and retrospec tive cast of countenance, was squatting upon his bundle on the hurricane deck, toasting his shins against the chimney, and apparently plunged into a state of profound meditation. He had been in the battle of Fort Donelson, and I began to interrogate him upon the subject. His philosophy was so much in the Falstaffian vein that I will give his views in his own words, as near as my memory serves me.

"Were you in the fight?"

"Had a little taste of it, sa."

"Stood your ground, did you?"

"No, sa, I runs."

"Run at the first fire, did you?"

"Yes, sa, and would hab run soona hab I knowd it was coming."

"Why, that wasn't very creditable to your courage."

"Dat isn't in my line, sa—cookin's my perfession."

"Well, but have you no regard for your reputation?"

"Reputation's nuffin to me by de side ob life."

"Do you consider your life worth more than other people's?"

"It's worth more to me, sa."

"Then you must value it very highly."

"Yes, sa, I does—more dan all dis world—more dan a million of dollars, sa, for what would dat be wuth to a man wid de bref out of him? Self-preserbashun am de fust law wid me, sa."

"But why should you act upon a different rule from other men?"

"'Cause, sa, different men sets different value upon darselves. My life is not in de market."

"But if you lost it, you would have the satisfaction of knowing that you died for your country."

"What satisfaction would dat be to me, when de power ob feelin' was gone?"

"Then patriotism and honor are nothing to you!"

"Nuffin whatever, sa—I regard dem as among de vanities."

"If our soldiers were like you, traitors might have broken up the Government without resistance."

"Yes, sa, dar would hab been no help for it. I wouldn't put my life in de scale 'ginst any gobernment dat eber existed, for no gobernment could replace de loss to me. 'Spect, dough, dat de gobernment safe if day all like me."

"Do you think any of your company would have missed you if you had been killed?"

"May be not, sa. A dead white man ain't much to dese sogers, let alone a dead nigga, but I'd a missed myself, and dat was de pint wid me."

It is safe to say that the dusky corpse of that African will never darken the field of carnage.

THE CORPORAL'S CONTRABAND TURKEY.

The soldier has a tedious time in wearing out the monotony of camp life, especially when the rations get low, or are of a quality that is not much better than it should be. But several thousand men, huddled together for many idle months, must needs have some fun; they will have it, too, and if it partakes of utility, so much the better. Fun and food they must have, and with three-fourths of their time to themselves, it would be a wonder if they did not concoct some plan that would bring them both. •

When Buell's army was camping in Kentucky, one of the boys came across a secesh barn, which appeared to be the head-quarters of a squad of rebel turkies. He accordingly reported to "Corporal Ben," who was generally the officer in command on such occasions.

"Good!" said Ben. "Them fellers are contraband, and we must make a reconnoissance in force, take a few prisoners and replenish our mess. Whose are they?"

"They belong to old Grudge, over there," replied Sam. "We shall have to be sly about it, for he's a mean old cuss, and would'nt let a fellow pick the bone of one o' them if he could help it. He's always on the watch."

"We'll try it," said Ben. "I'll get Duke to go along.

Accordingly when night came, the Corporal led his force be-fore the aforesaid barn and demanded a surrender. Silence, of course, gave consent, and the Corporal and his company pro-ceeded to take charge of the prisoners, while Duke was detailed to act as guard, and watch for the appearance of old Grudge.

Ben climbed up on the high beams and began to pass down the astonished turkies to Sam, who stood ready below to receive them. Ben had just handed down a worthy gobbler, when the proceedings were suspended by the hoarse baying of a sturdy bull dog, who came tearing down the lane.

"A dog!" cried the guard, in a very loud whisper.

"The dog, Ben," repeated Sam.

"Shoot him, Duke," commanded Ben.

"Nary shoot," said Duke. "It'll rout old Grudge." I must change my base of operations." And the guard stepped round the barn and climbed an apple tree. Sam, also looked this way and that way for a place of safety. But what is done must be done quickly, for the dog is already pouring his volleys of bark in at the very door. At this juncture Sam discovered the meal bin. In a twinkling he raised the lid and plunged himself head and ears in the yielding meal.

In the meantime the dog came in, and spying Ben perched upon the beam with the turkies, set up a renewed yelling. This condition of things could not long be endured. The repeated calls of the dog had routed the master, whose heavy foot-steps were already heard, plodding down the path. Sam raised the lid of his guard house and sung out:

"Hello! Ben!"

"Hello, yourself; what's the matter?"

"I'm in a predicament."

"It's a good thing, or the dog might eat you."

"What's to be done?"

"Keep dark, old Grudge is coming."

"How can I keep dark when I'm all white? I'm neck and
heels in the meal tub. Shoot that beggarly dog, and let's get out
of this."

"I darsn't," says Ben, "the old man is right here and I must
save it for him."

"O Lord!" exclaimed Sam, and down went the lid, just as
the light of a lantern relieved the darkness of the barn, and revealed the plethoric form of old Grudge, with his musket. His
wife was close at his heels. The dog's nose pointed in the direction of the Corporal, who was sitting, demurely, up among the
turkies.

"What are you doing up there, you thieving Yankee," said
Grudge, savagely.

"Roosting, you blubberly old Butternut.

> "Benighted, cold, and drenched with rain,
>   I sought this shelter,"—

Up among the turkies. What do *you* want?"

"Come down!" demanded the old man, at the same time
pointing the ominous looking musket at the corporal.

"I should think you might let a fellow rest," said Ben.

"The nasty, thieving Yankee!" exclaimed the old woman,
"to go fer to steal our turkies; better shoot him at once, and
it'll be a warnin' to the rest o' them fellers."

"Quit, quit," peeped a turkey.

"I second that motion," said Ben. "I say quit, and don't
point that old musket up here; it might go off and hurt some of
the turkies."

Click, went the trigger, which was followed by another order
more peremptory than the first.

"Hold on, old Butternut," said Ben, boldly, "you'd better not
shoot that. Don't you know that I've got a squad of men at the
end of the barn? The'll eat you up in two minutes. They're
all-fired hungry."

At this juncture Sam carefully raised the lid of his box and
crept out. He was white with meal from had to foot, and looked
exceedingly like a ghost. This suggested the idea to Ben, and
he continued, addressing old Grudge:

"Besides I'm one of them abolition Yankees that has the
power of raising the devil, and I'll do it in a minute, too, if you
don't put that gun out of the way."

Sam took the hint, and placing the turkey astride of his neck,
and grasping a leg in each hand, with a slow and measured step,

and a sepulchral groan, he stalked up towards the old folks with
the turkey's wings flapping furiously upon his shoulders. At
this moment the guard, who was in the apple tree and heard the
conversation, fired three of his five shots in quick succession.
Ben added another to the list, which happily passed through the
dog's heart.
"O, Lord!' shrieked the old woman, "thar's that thar ghost!"
"The devil!" cried the old man, and nervously discharged his
piece. The ball took effect on Sam's turkey, knocking it from
his shoulders and flooding his face with blood, which trickled
down his bosom, making little rills in the meal. The old
man supposing he had shot the devil's head clean away, was so
astonished, when Sam commenced singing:

"The devil he came to the farmer's one day."

that he turned and followed in the wake of his old woman, who
was screaming her way up towards the house. The boys took
a turkey in each hand, and with one accord hurried away, and
soon arrived safely in camp with their booty.
The next day old Grudge came into camp to see about his turkies. Ben spied him, and sidling up to him, whispered:
"Look here, old fellow. if you don't get out of this I'll have
the devil after you again!"
The old man concluded to take the turkey's advice, and quit.

ADVENTURES OF A DRUMMER BOY.

There was a drummer boy in one of the Ohio regiments, who
had a most remarkable faculty of getting into scrapes, and the
most surprising luck in getting out of them. On the day of the
fight Charlie concluded to go out and take a brush with the
whole rebel army, on his own hook. He persuaded another
drummer to go with him and share the glory. So with his
usual strategic brilliancy, Charlie posted himself between his
own and a rebel regiment, and had quite a lively time in
"changing front," as the storm of bullets came from one side
and the other. It was a perilous position; but they braced up
each other's courage with repeated laughing, and it was amusing
to observe the droll manner in which he described that "sickly
sort of laugh."
The fight was over, and Charlie and his companion in arms
escaped unhurt, and concluded to go back to camp and see about
their traps, but before they reached camp Charlie was taken
prisoner, and brought before a rebel lieutenant, who catechised
him in the following manner:

"Well, you d—d little Yankee cuss, what in the h—l are you doing here?"

"I want my knapsack," coolly answered Charlie.

"How many of you d—d Yankees are there over there?" said the Lieutenant savagely.

"I don't know, I did'nt count 'em. I guess I want my knap-sack," replied Charlie, demurely.

"But you can guess," said the Lieutenant.

"I don't know how many you fellers killed. Did you kill any?"

"I should reckon we did. But tell me how many you had before the fight."

"Well, about ten or twelve thousand," replied Charlie, carelessly.

"Don't lie to me, you little rascal;" said the officer savagely, at the same time drawing a revolver, "or I'll shoot you in a minute! Now tell me the truth, you little Yankee pup!"

"I don't know," said Charlie, and then, after a pause, during which he seemed to be summing up, to the astonishment of the the officer, he asked:

"How many men have *you* got?"

The rebel looked at him a moment as if endeavoring to make out the character of the boy, when feeling that this was too much for his chivalrous nature to bear, he faced Charlie about, gave him a tremendous kick in the rear, and said:

"Git! you little devil."

Charlie obeyed the order, and without further trouble got safely back to camp.

GENERAL ROUSSEAU AND THE REBELS.

A Southern gentleman came to General Rousseau, and requested permission to go beyond the Federal lines and visit his wife. He declared that he had never taken up arms against the Union, but he had aided and abetted those who had, and admitted that he was still a Secessionist.

"You can't go!" said the General.

"It seems very hard," replied Secesh, "that I can't go to see my wife."

"No harder for you than it is for me," returned the General. "I want to see my wife. You have compelled me to leave her by your infernal treason. You surely don't expect me to grant you a favor which your rebellious conduct prevents me from enjoying."

"Well, but, General—"

"It is useless to talk, sir. If you will go to work and assist me to return to my wife, I will do all I can to enable you to return to yours."

"What do you wish me to do, General?"

"I wish you to return to your allegiance, and, as far as lies in your power, to discountenance rebellion and treason."

"But, General, my conscience will not allow me to do that."

"*Neither, then,*" replied the Kentucky patriot, "will my conscience allow me to grant you favors which are due only to loyal men."

Of course as there was nothing further to be urged, the baffled rebel took up his hat and left. The General turned toward those who were sitting in his tent, and quietly remarked:

"When you have rendered these rebels fully sensible of how much they have lost by their rebellion, you have taken the first step toward making them loyal men."

Scarcely had the secesh gentleman taken his departure, when there came to the door of the tent a foppish fellow in striped summer clothing, with as mean a looking countenance as one often sees, even amongst the rebels. He held a piece of paper in his hand.

"General," said he, with much levity, insolence and noncha lance, "General, 1 could not get through your pickets, although I have here Gen. Buell's pass."

"Come in and sit down, sir," said the General; "I am glad to see you; I was just about to send out and have you arrested, and you have saved me the trouble."

The rebel's countenance instantly fell, and he began to stammer, "Why, General,"——

In a voice firm, determined, calm, and yet just angry enough to show that he was in earnest, the General interrupted him:

"I am told that you said to a crowd upon the street, that, rather than see the United States government restored throughout the South, you would see even your wife and children buried. If this can be proven against you, I shall send you at once to Fort Warren, as sure as there is a living God!"

Never could there be a more abject and contemptible looking specimen of a human being, than that rebel, as he appeared at the conclusion of this speech. The brazen impudence which at first sat upon his features was all gone. He turned first red, then deadly pale; he looked in-ludicrous dismay from one individual to another; he writhed, he swallowed, he choked.

"You are self-condemned, Dr. Martin," continued the General; "you are guilty of a heinous offence, and you know it. You had committed, by all laws, human and divine, the high crime of treason. You had accepted a commission as a surgeon in the rebel army, from the hands of Jeff Davis, whom you knew to bq at the head of a vast conspiracy for breaking up the government. You voluntarily offered yourself as a part of the machinery by means of which he expected to overturn the Republic, and destroy the lives of loyal men. You attached yourself, too, for the express purpose of giving aid and comfort to those who, for more than a year past, have been engaged in butchering our friends, our brothers and our fathers. Your famiy remained in this place, and, notwithstanding the presence of our troops, they have been treated with the utmost consideration and respect. You yourself, becoming tired of the rebel service, finally resigned; and knowing the clemency of the government against which you had been so long waging war, you unhesitatingly came into our midst. Instead of being at once arrested and hung as a traitor, you were cordially received, and treated in every respect like a gentleman. Were you not?"

"Oh, yes, General," stammered the rebel, "I have been treated very gentlemanly, indeed."

"You were not deprived of your liberty, were you?"

"Oh, no, I wasn't even required to give any parole, except my word."

"Certainly not," resumed the General; "notwithstanding your treason, we desired, if possible, to waken a sense of honor in your bosom, and consequently treated you as a man of honor, requiring you to give no bond for your good behavior, save your mere word. Freely as any loyal citizen you were permitted to go home, to enjoy the company of your family, and to mingle with your friends. And in return, how have you requited us? By using the most seditious and treasonable language; for some time, doubtless, within doors; until at last, insolently abusing your priviliges, or wholly unable to appreciate the wonderful magnanimity of the government in giving you your freedom, you go upon the street, collect a crowd around you, preach your treason to them openly, and wind up by declaring that you would rather bury your wife and children than see the authority of the National Government again restored! Now tell me, did the government ever harm you in any way?"

"No," replied the guilty rebel, "I can't say that it ever did."

"And yet you made war upon it, and, even after it had given you blessings for cursings, sought to stir up the devil in your neighbors' hearts, by telling them you would rather bury your wife and children than see it resume its rightful authority over the rebellious States!"

During the entire castigation, the doctor writhed and twisted like a serpent in the talons of an eagle. Rallying himself somewhat at last, he made a feeble attempt at a denial, and said he could not remember having ever made use of such language. "My information," replied the General, "will not allow me to

doubt your guilt. Consider yourself under arrest; but, as I
have not time to investigate the matter more fully now, I will
permit you to go home to your family and spend the night.
Return to-morrow morning at nine o'clock, when you shall be
confronted with the witnesses who accuse you." In consequence
of the accusation not being as grave as was at first supposed,
this rebellious subject was suffered to remain by taking the oath
of allegiance.

A SAD MISTAKE.

When the Federal forces first took possession of the two
houses in Casey's old camp, they found them filled with wounded,
both rebel and Union. The Surgeon of the Fifth Excelsior was
attending to them on Monday morning, and reports a curious
conversation he had with one of them. He was the first Union
surgeon they had seen. One poor fellow was lying covered with
a Secesh blanket, with his face to the wall. Taking him for a
Secesh, the Surgeon said:

"My boy, what tempted you to fight against us?"

"I was impressed, sir," answered the soldier dolefully.

"Drafted, were you?"

"Yes, sir. I did'nt want to come, but they drafted me, and I
could'nt help it."

"What is your regiment?" kindly inquired the Surgeon.

"ONE HUNDREDTH NEW YORK."

"So they are drafting in New York, are they?"

"Yes sir."

The mistake had been mutual. The soldier had taken the
surgeon for a Secessionist, (not seeing his uniform,) and only
realized the status of affairs when told that it was a tolerably
large lie even for a Secessionist to swallow. The chagrin of the
mendacious coward at his mistake, can better be imagined than
described.

SOUTHERN LOYALTY.

The following incident is a fair specimen of the value of the
oath of allegiance:

When General Robert Mitchell was in Jacinto, he learned
that a band of Guerrillas had their headquarters at a little place
called Bay Springs, twenty miles further south, where there was
a large cotton factory belonging Northern man, whom they

had driven away, and whose factory they were running on Confederate account. By a detour of forty miles, General Mitchell, with a small force, came up on the south side of them and captured some twenty prisoners, killing a few in the melee. He then took from the machinery of the factory some small, but important wheels, which can be replaced only by a Northern machinist, and loaded up all the cotton his wagons would hold, and started for Jacinto. Night overtook him near the plantation of an old fellow who had been very active for a week, or so, in peddling onions and other delicacies through the camp, and whose loyalty General Mitchell had suspected, notwithstanding his oath. He determined to test it, and accordingly sent forward a portion of his staff to ask entertainment for General Price, of the rebel army, and his staff, for the night. The plot worked admirably. Old Loyalty was delighted to see General Price, and entertained him with a detailed account of the Federal camp at Jacinto, the number of men, and the general strength of the place. He was helped in his information by two sons and a nephew, nearly grown, who offered to conduct General Price to Jacinto in the morning, and point out the exact position of each regiment and battery.

"And, now," said General Price, "there is another thing quite as important as this information. We must know who are our real friends in this vicinity and whom we can trust. We don't care a d—n how often they swear to the Feds—that is nothing. We want men who, while they swear to the Feds, feed and clothe the Confederates." So old Loyalty gave the names of his principal neighbors as of that stripe, detailing with great care their labors in behalf of the rebel army, while acting as peddlers in the Federal camp, all of which General Price took down in his book of remembrance.

At a late hour they retired to bed, but not to sleep much. All parties were too well pleased with the incidents of the night. In the morning, however, to the surprise of the old planter, he found his house guarded by the blue pants, and about twenty Butternuts also under guard, in his yard, and over in the field was a little army of the men whom he had taken to be at Jacinto. The old man and the boys were immediately placed under a strong guard.

The next night one of the neighbors was waited upon by a squad of soldiers. He plead that he had taken the oath—that he was loyal, and that *the Constitution protected him!*

"But what about that band of guerrillas you boarded last week?" said the Corporal.

"I never!" exclaimed the old man.

"I say, old fellow," continued his tormentor, "did that captain pay you for that nice bay he took away?"

3

"No, he never!" continued the old fellow, who by this time was too full of confusion to explain further.

"Did he give you a note?" still persisted the officer.

"No, he never!"

By this time southern pluck got the ascendency, and the rebel boldly inquired:

"How did you learn about my private business? What traitor has betrayed me into your hands?"

"It is no difference, sir," replied the officer, "you will prepare to go with us to Jacinto, and while we are about it, as we shall have to clothe you, we may as well take a little of your cotton."

So onion peddler No. 2 lost his liberty and his cotton.

STONEWALL JACKSON.

The notorious rebel General, Thomas Jefferson Jackson, got the *sobriquet* of "Stonewall," from the fact of his fighting from behind a stone wall in one of the battles of Virginia. He is a brave, shrewd General, and as he has won such notoriety in the rebel cause, a slight sketch of his character and cunning may not be uninteresting.

He is described as a "slow man," intellectually, even dull. Some say he was a tedious professor, and all agree that he has a creeping look. And yet, if you ask them what they mean by that, they say they don't know; "all they do know is, that he is as obstinate as a mule, and plucky as a bull dog," which means just nothing of a man whose prime quality is celerity, quick conclusions, and startling execution; who, as a soldier, is as rapid as he is wary, abounding in surprises, brave almost to rashness, and inventive almost to romance.

As for his outer man, he looks at least seven years older than he is—his height about five feet ten inches; his figure is thick set, square shouldered, and decidedly clumsy; his gait very awkward, stooping, and with long strides. He often walks with his head somewhat on one side, and his eyes fixed on the ground, imparting to his whole appearance that abstracted quality which young ladies describe as "absent minded." A lady who has known him long and well, remarks that she never saw him on horseback without laughing. Short stirrups, knees cramped up, heels stuck out behind, and chin on his breast—a most unmilitary phenomenon. In society he is quiet, but cheerful; not loquacious, but intelligent and shrewd; in religion, the bluest kind of a Presbyterian, and extremely strict in his church observances. In Winchester he took a very active part in revivals, and habitually led the "Union Prayer Meetings."

To illustrate the popularity of the man: For some reason, which has never been made public, the expediency of removing him from his command was at one-time freely discussed in the Confederate Cabinet, and all but two members favored the motion. These two, arguing that a man of such exemplary modesty, and yet of such intense religious enthusiasm and indomitable firmness, *must* possess those moral elements which, combined with his military education and experience, should constitute a great General. Their opposition served to postpone a decision, and the motion was held under consideration. Meantime, 'the people of the valley got wind of the affair, and with a great outcry of indignation and threats so assailed the powers at Richmond, that the question was dropped "like a hot potato." It was about this time that Jackson sent to Richmond his Rebel-famous dispatch—"Send me more men and no orders, or more orders and no men."

Such is the Rebel Napoleon, for whom his people venture to claim that in four weeks he has marched three hundred and fifty miles, and won four victories—that he has crippled or dispersed the forces of Milroy and Schenck at McDowell, Banks at Front Royal and Winchester, Fremont at Cross Keys, and Shields at Port Republic —that he held McDowell in check to take care of Washington and Maryland, and monopolizes, for the amusement of the world, the attention of six distinguished Generals.

Nevertheless, when he fell back to Winchester from pursuing Banks, he said to the people there: "When we left you last March, we promised to return—and here we are. Now, with much more confidence, we promise to return again, and soon. Only be prudent and patient."

And to the women: "When the Union troops come in again, as they will, do not forget yourselves."

The surgeon of one of the Indiana regiments, and two of his brother officers, were captured by a party of Ashby's cavalry and taken before Jackson. Immediately on hearing their names he said: "It was you, gentlemen, who lately saved the property of a dear friend of mine in the valley from the fury of your own men. I thank you. Have you any means of transportation back to your regiment?"

"We have not, General."

He then gave them horses, an escort, and $100, and courteously dismissed them on their parole.

The chivalry of Richmond descend, at times, to the vulgar relaxation of street jokes, as thus:

"Well, Rebel, are you ready to be pushed to that wall?"

"What wall?"

"Stonewall."

"Where is it?"

"Right in front of the last ditch."

One thing is certain—Jackson is equally eminent as a strategist and tactitian. He handles his army like a whip, making it crack in out-of-the-way corners where you scarcely thought the lash would reach.

Colonel Ford had a conversation of an hour or more with him, and he represents him as a most cool and imperturbable personage. Jackson said the rebels did not intend to damage anything in Maryland except the Baltimore and Ohio Railroad, which they considered as contraband of war. They intended no harm to the people of the North, and only desired to impress upon them and the whole world their ability to achieve their independence. While they were in conversation an orderly rode rapidly across the bridge, and said to Gen. Jackson:

"I am ordered, by General McLaws, to report to you that General McClellan is within six miles, with an immense army."

Jackson took no notice of the orderly, apparently, and continued his conversation; but, when the orderly had turned away Jackson called after him with the question:

"Has McClellan any baggage train, or drove of cattle?"

"He has, sir," replied the orderly.

"Very well," he said, "my men are hungry, and we can whip any army that is followed by a drove of cattle."

A rather frank admission of the famishing condition of the rebel army.

A KEEN ANSWER.

The Indian rebellion in Minnesota is generally supposed to have been prompted by rebel authority, although the chivalry generally disclaim being privy to any such barbarities. Occasionally, however, a word will leak out which shows that they know more about it than they are willing to acknowledge.

General Wm. W. Morris had for his guests the Marquis of Huntingdon and some of the British navy officers. In the course of conversation one of them inquired of the General whether the employment of parolled prisoners taken at Harper's Ferry against the Indians was not a violation of the parol.

"That would depend upon the character of the parol," said the General. "If it is not to take up arms against the rebels till exchanged, and so I understand it to be, I should think their being employed against the Indians would not be a violation of the terms of the engagement."

A UNION WOMAN.

One of the enrolling marshals of Philadelphia stopped at a lady's house to hunt up all the inmates liable to military duty. "Have you any men here, ma'am?" inquired the officer gruffly.

"No," answered the lady, in the same tone.

"Have you no husband, ma'am?"

"No."

"Nor brothers?"

"No."

"Perhaps you have a son, ma'am?"

"Well, what of it?"

"I should like to know where he is."

"Well, he isn't here."

"So I see, ma'am. Pray, where is he?"

"In the Union army, where you ought to be."

The marshal did not further interrogate the lady.

TERRIBLE EXECUTION OF TEN GUERRILLAS.

An eye-witness tells the following thrilling story, which illustrates the rigid discipline that is necessary in times of war:

After looking around through a very clean camp of some blue-capped recruits, and a very dirty camp of an old regiment that had been at Shiloh, I returned to the headquarters, when I found the General and his staff just mounting to go to the execution ground. Presently came the solemn roll of the muffled drum, and then appeared the head of a column of soldiers, moving over the hill at a slow pace. Going toward them, I found it was the execution party with the condemned men. First, a prisoner—hard, desperate face, yet showing intelligence —then a file of soldiers six abreast, and so on down the column, until the rear was brought up by the regiment of infantry, the recruits, and some cavalry clad in homespun, that, but for their arms, I should have supposed were Secesh prisoners, but found they were militia of Missouri, called out by their Governor to put down guerrillas.

The execution ground was about half a mile from the town, and when I reached there I found the troops drawn up on three sides of a square, while the fourth was occupied by the condemned and the firing parties. A long line of mounted sentinels kept back the too-curious crowd, but a word from a polite little Major, who had previously seen me at the headquarters, admitted me, and I took my place near the General and his Staff, in one corner of the square. After some time occupied in the preliminary preparations, each prisoner was blindfolded, and knelt in front of his own execution party. A venerable-looking, gray-headed Chaplain now stepped out from among the staff, and in a short, fervent prayer, commended the souls of these poor wretches to the mercy of the God before whom they would shortly appear. Every thing was as still as death. The perfect hush, if I may say so, was painfully distinct, and I could see, even under the grave, stern face of the General, a softening look, as if he was still struggling between duty and mercy.

For a moment the silence was awful; then came the clear tone of command of the officer of the day:

"Ready; aim; fire!"

A rattling discharge; a puff of smoke; a groan; and all was over. The ten had paid the penalty of their broken oaths. For a moment all was hushed, as before, and then you could almost hear the long drawn breath of relief. The bright sun shone as calmly and clearly as before, but shone on ten corpses stiff and stark, where a moment before were ten men in the full flush of physical health.

A surgeon stepped from the lines and walked along, examining each body as he passed, then stepped up to the General with a stiff military salute:

"They are all dead, Sir."

"Very well, Sir," replied the General, without the change of a muscle, not the slightest relaxing of the outward sternness, and yet, I thought, a moment ago, you might have saved their lives. Truly, here is a man whose sense of duty would carry him through any thing, and I felt disappointed that he exhibited no more feeling. But a moment after, as he turned to mount his horse, I heard him say to one of his staff, "God in mercy spare me such a duty as that again, and yet mercy to those men is the harshest cruelty to the whole people of this State."

REBEL GRATITUDE.

When, from blind motives, a good man enters into a wicked cause, as is this rebellion, he must needs let some of his better nature leak out occasionally. Several Union prisoners were brought before Colonel Gardiner, who, as soon as he beheld them, ordered them to be immediately and unconditionally released, and made each man a handsome present.

At the battle of Bull Run, Colonel Gardiner was wounded and left on the field to die. These men found him, gave him water from their canteens, and otherwise ministered to his wants, thus restoring him to life. This is an evidence of how kindness subdues even your enemies on the battle field.

A YANKEE TRICK.

A shrewd stratagem was successfully employed by Capt. Gregory, of the United States brig Bohio, employed on blockading duty in the Gulf of Mexico. A schooner was discovered far away in the distance, which, on the Bohio displaying the Stars and Stripes, tried to escape. All sail was crowded on the Bohio, but without gaining on the strange craft, which proved to be a fast sailer, and beyond the reach of the Bohio's guns. The Bohio's sails were then wet, when a slight gain was made. At last the Captain resorted to strategy, and rigged a "smoke stack" amidships, and built a fire, and soon had "steam on." As soon as the stranger saw this she hove to, thinking the Bohio was a steamer and would soon catch her. On boarding her she was found to be the Henry Travers, of Nassau, N. P., with a cargo of coffee and soap, with which she intended to run the blockade. she made a nice prize, worth $50,000.

THE FATE OF ZOLLICOFFER.

At the battle of Mill Spring, two mounted officers came trotting along the right flank of the 4th Kentucky, and noticing their firing upon the rebels near by, shouted:

"Don't fire on your friends; they are Mississippians."

At this juncture Colonel Fry came up to the front of his regiment, when one of the officers fired upon him, the ball passing close to his head. At a glance, Colonel Fry recognized, in the other, General Zollicoffer. In a twinkling he pulled out his revolver and fired at the rebel chieftain, putting a bullet through his breast, and causing his fall from the horse and instant death. The rebel aid put spurs to his horse, and quickly spread the news of the fall of his General among the rebels.

Zollicoffer's body lay for nearly three days on the ground, in front of the tent of the sutler of the 10th Kentucky, wrapped in a blanket. He was a man of middle height, light hair, rather long features, well formed profile, and rather pleasant expression of countenance, which grim death did not altogether destroy. His skin was beautifully white and clear. He had his beard shaved off on the evening before the battle, probably in order to be less easily recognized. It was a pity that his remains were outrageously treated by the thousands of soldiers and citizens that flocked to see them. Not only was all of his hair cut off close to the skull, but the body was stripped of its clothing. When killed, he had on a white rubber coat, under which he wore a full General's uniform. The rubber coat, the uniform, the boots, his over and undershirt, and even his socks, were either carried off whole, or gradually cut off in pieces. On Tuesday evening the body was almost naked. This kind of curiosity-hunting borders on vandalism. The warm temperature that prevailed after the battle hastened the decomposition of the remains. Then was literally "treason smelling to heaven." What a horrid end of a once high and honorable career.

NOVEL AMMUNITION.

During the battle of Antietam, broken railroad iron, blacksmith's tools, hammers, chisels, etc., were fired at us from rebel cannon. Some of these missiles made a peculiar noise, resembling "which-away, which-away," by which our men came to distinguish them from regular shot and shell, and as they heard them approaching they would cry "turkey! turkey coming!" and fall flat to avoid them. One of the artillerists, a German, when he saw the tools falling around him, exclaimed :

"My Gott! we shall have the blacksmith's shop to come next!"

LOST MULES RECOVERED, WITH INTEREST.

When the Union troops first received their teams, at Paducah, they had some difficulty in procuring forage, so the mules were turned loose. From time to time these mules were missing, until at last Uncle Sam found himself minus some twenty-five or thirty. Those which strayed away were caught up by rebel speculators, and taken to Blandville, where they had accumulated about fifty stolen and purchased animals, which were under the charge of half a dozen keepers. Two privates of the 14th Illinois, hearing of the whereabouts of the stock, asked General Smith's permission to go and get them, which, with some misgivings, the General granted.

The two boys, dressing themselves in the garb f Kentucky farmers, went and surveyed the field and fold, and set to work. They had whisky with them, such whisky as the rebels like to get drunk on—good old Bourbon—and the first object was to get them as comfortably tight as possible. When this was accomplished, which was no difficult matter, the boys went to the mule yard, let down the bars, mounted two of the best, and, without saddle or bridle, started for Paducah, the whole lot of mules following at a breakneck pace, and braying in the most diabolical chorus.

This music somewhat sobered the rebel keepers, who when they discovered the trick, gave chase; but not deeming it prudent to venture too close to the Union lines, they halted, held council, and concluded to return home and make the best of their Bourbon sell; while the boys rode furiously into camp with their shrieking retinue, and reported to General Smith.

"Well, boys, what luck?" asked the General.

"We got 'em good, sure, and more too," said one.

"Ah!" said the General, "how many did you get?"

"Well, about forty, I reckon; haint counted 'em yet," said the soldier.

"But that is more than we have lost. You didn't steal any, I hope?" said the General, chidingly.

"Steal!" exclaimed the soldier, "Kr—istopher! steal! No sirree; but you see we didn't have time to put up the bars, after we got ourn out, and the d—d things would foller!"

The General was astonished, both at the trick and the impious language; and, putting on a long face, he sternly lectured the soldier for using profane language in the presence of a general officer.

The soldier took the lecture quite uneasily, twirling his hat nervously, and, when the General concluded, apologized as follows:

"You see, General, we've had to cuss the d—d things all day to get 'em into camp, and it's devilish hard to quit off all of a sudden!"

The General relaxed the rigidity of his features, and would have laughed had discipline permitted. In consideration, however, of the twenty-five mules and "more too," he generously dismissed the boys without an order for arrest. The boys were glad to get off so easily; but they declared, as they closed the door, that "such a pious old cuss had no business to be round among soldiers."

DEATH OF GEN. NELSON.

Brigadier General Jeff. C. Davis reported to Major General Nelson that he had the brigade, assigned to his command, ready for service, and desired to know if he could get arms for them.

"How many men have you?" asked Nelson.

"About 2,500, sir," replied Davis.

"*About* 2,500! *About!*" answered Nelson, savagely. "You a regular officer, and report *about* the number of men in your command! Don't you know, sir, you should report the exact number?"

4

"But, General," replied Davis, "I didn't expect to get the arms now; I only wanted to know if I could get them, and when; and, having learned that, I would ascertain the exact number and draw accordingly."

"*About* 2,500," grumbled Nelson. "I suspend you from your command, and order you to report to General Wright, and I've a d—d mind to send you out of the city with a provost guard!"

Subsequently they again met at the Galt House, in Louisville, when General Davis asked an explanation, and remarked:

"General Nelson, I am a general officer, and as such I wish to be treated."

Nelson's language was very profane and insulting on this occasion.

"You do not deserve it, sir," he replied, "when you are ignorant of the number of your men."

"But, General, I wish an explanation—I demand it," persisted Davis.

"You've got all you deserve, you d—d puppy!" replied Nelson, at the same time slapping Davis in the face, while he continued his abuse.

The stinging blow and the stinging language were too much for the spirited nature of General Davis. He immediately turned to a friend, borrowed a pistol, and, stepping up to his superior, bid him defend himself, and, as Nelson turned, he fired, the ball passing through his body.

Nelson lived but twenty minutes, and these last twenty, precious moments of his life, were passed in religious exercises with the Rev. Mr. Talbott.

General Nelson was a brave soldier, but had an irritable temper, which the circumstances of his maritime life had in no way tended to soften. It is an old adage that "He who would govern others must first learn to govern himself." Had General Nelson adopted this principle in early life, he might still have been doing honor to himself and service to his country. General Davis was arrested, but subsequently released and assigned to his command.

A ZOO-ZOO JOKE.

The Zouaves are notorious for their jokes, and sometimes they are cracked to some practical purpose. One of them, who had formerly been a typo in Chicago, was on picket duty one day, when an F. F. V., with rather more than the usual pomposity of his race, rode up in a carriage from the direction of Alexandria, driven, of course, by his servant. Zoo-Zoo stepped

"But is it not a violation of the *spirit* of the parol?" said one.

"I do not see it," replied the General.

"But," said the other, "would not the United States be compelled to employ against the Indians a portion of the force they are now employing against the Confederates, if their parolled prisoners could not be so used?"

"Certainly," replied the General, "but the rebels do not claim the Indians as their allies, and the argument is not, therefore, tenable."

"But suppose you were at war with us?"

"The same rule would hold good."

"If we were the allies of the Confederates?"

"That," replied the General, earnestly, "would alter the case very materially; but in that event we might not need the assistance of parolled prisoners!"

The visitors did not press the subject further, for the manner of the General gave an appreciative zest to his words. It must be remembered that the foreigners are themselves the authors of these stories, which they told with no little glee, as the result of a discomfiture they had not looked for.

YANKEE HORNS.

The lower classes of Rebeldom have strange notions of the Yankees. Some of them are taught to believe that the Yankee is a curiosity—a sort of *lusus naturæ*, who wears horns, and has bristly hair all over his body, cloven feet, etc. A traveler tells the following:

A staving ride of nine miles brought us to the farm-house of Jerry Ballou, a decent old man, who gave us a supper, a good bed, and a chance to nurse my wounded man. As we rode up, his little daughter looked curiously at me.

"Paw, is that a Yankee?"

"Yes, little dear," said I, "and if I had known I was coming to make you a visit, I should have worn my horns."

The child looked wonders at me, and, eyeing me from head to foot, innocently remarked:

"Well, I don't see but you look like people when you hain't got your horns on."

REBEL LIBERALITY.

The rebels were extremely liberal about paying for everything, in their bogus and baseless scrip; in fact, they frequently forced this upon the people, and compelled them to take large quantities of it whether they would or no.

During a rebel raid into Kentucky they seized a horse belonging to a Union man.

"What is he worth?" they demanded.

"One hundred dollars," replied the man.

"O," said they, "that is entirely too cheap; we will give you two hundred." Upon this they pulled out two hundred dollars of Confederate scrip and handed it toward him.

"Have you no other money?" he asked.

"None," was the reply.

"Very well," said he, "you are welcome to the horse; I do not want your money."

"But you must take it," said they, "or we will immediately arrest you for treason."

Upon this he accepted it, and they moved off with his horse. This, and hundreds of similar incidents, show that one grand object of the rebel raid in Kentucky, was to force vast quantities of this worthless scrip upon the people, and thus enlist the pecuniary interests of a large class of them in favor of their bogus government.

A CLERGYMAN INDUCES A BURGLAR TO GO TO THE WARS.

An eminent Presbyterian clergyman of Philadelphia, stopping at one of our first-class hotels, was awakened in the night by a noise in his room. Supposing it was caused by a young friend who shared the room, he called to him by name. Receiving no answer, he raised his head and saw, by the faint light of the moon, that his companion was in bed, and that the noise was caused by a figure whose shadowy outline he saw in another part of the room. Springing from his bed, and rushing upon the intruder, the clerical gentleman exclaimed:

"What are you doing in my room?"

"Robbing you," promptly and coolly answered the visitor.

The young man being by this time awakened, and having lighted the gas, our divine proceeded to examine the capture that he had made. Placing his hand upon his shoulder, and bending on the thief a look that "took the measure of his soul," he interrogated him concerning his course of life, and the causes that had thus strangely brought them together. After a long conversation the clergyman had so charmed the burglar and won his affection, that he begged to be taken into his service, saying he would be honest, and follow him to the end of the earth.

Our friend, not desiring to have a follower whose acquaintance had been so strangely made, and wishing at the same time to give the culprit a chance for reform, promised that he would not deliver him to justice if he would enter the army, and agreed that, in the morning, he would make the necessary arrangements for his enlistment. The thief left, with the promise that, at a certain hour the next day, he would meet the clergyman at the hotel, and go with him to the nearest recruiting station.

Strange as it may appear, the burglar was prompt at keeping his appointment, and accompanied his new friend to the rendezvous, was enrolled, inspected, mustered in, uniformed, and the same afternoon left for his regiment with the Army of the Potomac, showering thanks upon the head of his strangely acquired benefactor.

CLERICAL BON MOT.

When at dinner, the other day, at the residence of a mutual friend, Bishop Rosecrans being at the table, the conversation naturally turned upon th cent fight at Iuka, under command of his brother, General Rosecrans.

"It would seem to me, Bishop, that you and your brother, the General, are engaged in very different callings," remarked a gentleman to his worship.

"Yes, it *appears* so," returned the Bishop. "And yet," he continued, "we are both *fighting* men. While the General is wielding 'the sword of the flesh,' I trust that I am using 'the sword of the Spirit.' He is fighting the rebels, and I am fighting the spirits of darkness. There is this difference in the terms of our service: he is fighting with *Price*, while I am fighting without price."

A THRILLING ROMANCE.

The case of private Scott, killed in the fight near Lee's Mills, is worthy of being recorded. He was court martialed for sleeping on his post, out near Chain Bridge, on the Upper Potomac. He was convicted; the sentence was death; the finding was approved of by the General, and the day fixed for his execution. He was a youth of more than ordinary intel igence; he did not beg for pardon, but was willing to meet his fate. The time drew near; the stern necessity of war required that an example should be made of some one: his was an aggravated case. But the case reached the ears of the President; he resolved to save him; he signed a pardon and sent it out; the day came. "Suppose," thought the President, "my pardon has not reached him." The telegraph was called into reqisition; an answer did not come promptly. "Bring up my carriage," he ordered. It came, and soon the important State papers were dropped, and, through the hot, broiling sun and dusty roads, he rode to the camp, about ten miles, and saw that the soldier was saved! He has doubtless forgotten the incident, but the soldier did not. When the 3rd Vermont charged upon the rifle pits, the enemy poured a volley upon them. The first man who fell, with six bullets in his body, was Wm. Scott, of Company K. His comrades caught him up, and, as his life-blood ebbed away, he raised to heaven, amid the din of war, the cries of the dying, and the shouts of the enemy, a prayer for the President; and as he died he remarked to his comrade that he had shown he was no coward and not afraid to die.

He was interred, in the presence of his regiment, in a little grove about two miles to the rear of the Rebel fort, in the center of a group of holly and vines; a few cherry trees, in full bloom, are scattered around the edge. In digging his grave, a skull and bones were found, and metal buttons, showing that the identical spot had been used in the Revolutionary war for our fathers who fell in the same cause. The Chaplain narrated the circumstance to the boys, who stood around with uncovered heads. He prayed for the President, and paid a most glowing tribute to his noble heart. The tears started in their eyes as the clods of earth were thrown upon him in his narrow grave, where he lay shrouded in his coat and blanket.

The men separated; in a few minutes all were engaged in something around the camp, as though nothing unusual had happened; but that scene will live upon their memories while life lasts; the calm look of Scott's face, the seeming look of satisfaction he felt, still lingered; and could the President have seen him, he would have felt that his act of mercy had been wisely bestowed.

GENERAL TILGHMAN LIONIZED.

When General Tilghman was taken prisoner, Commodore Foote asked him why he wished to fight against the "old flag?"

"It *was* hard," he replied, "but I had to go with my people."

One of the reporters, who was preparing a ▬▬▬▬tch, asked him: "How do you spell your name, General?"

"Sir," he answered, "I do not desire to have my name appear in this matter, in any newspaper connection whatever. If Gen.

Grant sees fit to use it in his official dispatches, I have no objection, Sir; but I do not wish to have it in the newspapers."

"I merely asked it," persisted the reporter, "to mention as one among the prisoners captured,"

"You will oblige me, Sir," reiterated the General, with a waive of the hand and a this-settles-the-matter-air, "by not giving my name in any newspaper connection whatever."

The reporter withdrew, a good deal amused. Gen. Tilghman must have unique ideas on the subject of journalism to suppose that a lion of his dimensions would not be catalogued.

IMPORTANT INTERVIEW WITH LOYAL INDIANS.

The importance of the interview between Commissioner Dole and the Chiefs of the Seminoles, Creeks, Iowas and Delawares, loyal Indians, can hardly be over-estimated.

The Indians expressed great pleasure in seeing Commisioner Dole. The Southern Indians said their people had been driven from home and were suffering.

Mr. Dole.—"Government did not expect the Indians to enter this contest at all. Now that the rebel portion of them have entered the field, the Great Father will march his troops into your country. Colonel Coffin and the Agents will go with you, and will assist you in enlisting your loyal men. Your enlistment is not done for our advantage only; it will inure to your own benefit. The country appreciates your services. We honor you. You are in our hearts."

"One party tell that John Ross is for the Union, and one that he is not."

Opothleyoholo.—"Both are probably right. Ross made a sham treaty with Albert Pike to save trouble. Ross is like a man lying on his belly, watching the opportunity to turn over. When the Northern troops come within hearing he will turn over."

Dole.—"You did not, and our people remember you. But we hope you will manifest no revenge."

Opothleyoholo.—"The rebel Indians are like a cross, bad slut. The best way to end the breed is to kill the slut."

Dole.—"The leaders and plotters of treason only should suffer."

Opothleyoholo.—"That's just what I think. Burn over a bad field of grass and it will spring up again. It must be torn up by the roots, even if some good blades suffer. The educated part of our tribes is the worst. I am glad General Lane is going down with us. He knows our wants. I hope the Government money will be paid us."

Dole.—"We can not pay you until we know who of you are Union and who rebel."

Opothleyoholo.—"Those left back there are not loyal; we asked them to fight; we asked them to come up to Kansas; they did neither. They didn't help us in our time of trouble, and we won't help them. They turned against the Government with their eyes open. If we gain our land, we should have it and they nothing. We have talked it over among ourselves, and concluded not to do any thing for them."

Dole.—"We cannot pay you until all your chiefs are together, or substitutes elected, and a council held."

Opothleyoholo.—"All those left back there are secesh."

Dole.—"I have not the power to use the money except in a legal and regular way. We will take care of you, and the delay in paying you will be as brief as possible."

Opothleyoholo.—The Creeks have fifteen hundred warriors who want to fight for the Union."

Aluktustenuke (Chief of the Seminoles).—"We have two hundred and sixty warriors, and they will fight for the Great Father."

Major Burbank (Agent of the Iowas).—There are about fifty warriors in the tribe; they want to know on what conditions they can raise one hundred and fifty men, if they unite with the Otoes, who speak the same language."

White Cloud acted as the interpreter.

Dole.—"The Great Father has decided to accept your services to put down this rebellion in case it is your pleasure to give your services. You will not be expected to join white men unless they are arrayed against loyal Indians. will receive the same pay as white men. The Government is not horses. The red man is said to be fleet on foot, and seems to me that you ought to be able to go the same as white men. We should not have called upon you at all had not your own brothers been driven from their homes. You go to their assistance, not ours."

Lagarash.—"We came down for our Nation to find out how it was, and we want to hear *the straight.* I depend on my Nation; I sit with my ear open to hear what they will do."

Dole.—"You see before you Opothleyoholo, who has already been fighting for the Union; now, what will you do?"

Lagarash.—"I can not tell what they will do; I am ready."

Mawhee.—"I only wait for my neighbors."

Towhee.—"It depends upon the Nation."

Dole.—"Unless the Chiefs speak out the warriors will refuse to do so. Will you yourselves urge your people to act?"

Lagarash.—"We want to know how long the war is to be, and in what way we are to fight ?"

Dole.—Not more than twelve months. As to the manner of fighting—you can all draw a bead at two hundred yards. *Your* way of fighting will answer our purpose."

Lagarash.—"We want to go down there on horseback."

Dole.—" We are going to send twenty thousand white men on foot."

Lagarash.—"Yes, that's the way white men fight; Indians don't. When we fight, we don't fight all the time; we don't want to fight so long. I think we can end the war in one battle."

Dole.—"That will suit us. You are are a large, noble, and brave set of men. Let me hear you say that you will be brave warriors, whether others are or not."

Lagarash.—"I told you that whatever my Father wanted me to do I would do."

Mr. Dole arose and shook hands with the Iowa warrior. All present arose with them, and expressed their approbation by silent eloquence.

Dole.—"When you go home, tell your warriors to get ready, and prepare to be as brave as in former times. We may not want you for some time. Tell them that your brother red men have been driven from their homes, and they need your assistance. If only white men were at war we should not call upon you."

A KEEN PICKET.—ENCOUNTER OF WITS.

At times, the rebels are quite communicative, as the following dialogue, which occurred at Yorktown, between Jos. D., of Leeds, Wis., and one of the rebels, when within ten rods of each other, will show:

The parties were separated by a low, deep swale, covered with water and thick brush, and were unable to discover each other's person. Joe, hearing a noise on the other side, yelled out, in a loud voice:

"Hallo, Mike! have you got any tobacco ?"

Secesh—(with a strong Hibernian accent)—"Yes, be jabbers, and whisky, too."

Joe.—Come over and we'll have a quiet smoke."

"I'll meet you half way."

Joe agreed to say so, and advanced some distance through brush and water, and then stopped.

Secesh.—"Where the divil are ye? Are ye comin' ?"

Joe.—"I'm half way now. Can't go any further without swimming."

Secesh.—"Haven't ye a boat?"

Joe.—"No, I have not."

Secesh.—"Where's yer gunboat?"

Joe.—"Down taking care of the Merrimac."

Secesh.—"Then come over in that big balloon."

[Much laughter along the rebel lines.]

Joe.—"Have you a boat?"

Secesh.—"I have, sure, and I'm coming over."

Joe then inquires the news of the day, and if his companies had a Norfolk *Day Book.*

Secesh.—"I have. Have you got a *Tribune?*"

Joe.—"I have not."

Secesh.—Where is Gen. Buell?"

Joe.—"Buell's all right, and surrounds Beauregard."

Secesh.—"Where's Gen. Prentiss?"

Joe.—"Where's Johnston?"

[Another rebel laugh.]

Joe.—"How about Island No. 10?"

Secesh.—"That's evacuated."

Joë.—"How is it that you left 100 guns and 6,000 prisoners?"

Secesh.—"Sure, such prisoners are not of much account."

Joe.—"How about Fort Pulaski?"

Secesh.—"That be blowed! It was only a rebel sand bank. But tell me what made ye leave Bull Run?"

Dick B.—(Union.)—We had marching orders?"

This caused great laughter among the rebels, some exclaiming "Bully Boy!"

Dick B.—"Where's Zollicoffer?"

Secesh.—"Gone up the spout."

Joe.—"Why don't you come over?"

Secesh.—"Can't get through the brush."

At this moment a rebel bullet came whizzing over by our men, and Joe angrily inquired who fired.

Secesh.—"Some fool over this way."

An order was then issued to cease firing.

Joe.—"Ain't you coming? What regiment do you belong to?"

Secesh.—"Eighteenth Florida. What regiment do you?"

Joe.—"Berdan's First Regiment Sharpshooters."

Some of his comrades here warned him to look out.

Secesh.—"Would you shoot a fellow?"

Joe.—"No; but I will stack arms and smoke with you, if you will come over."

Here a rebel officer ordered him back, and the Secessionist refused to communicate further.

into the road, holding his bayonet in such a way as to threaten horse, negro and white man at one charge, and roared out:

"Tickets!"

Chivalry turned up his lip, turned down his brow, and by other gestures indicated his contempt for such "mud sills" as the soldier before him, ending by handing his pass over to the darkie and motioning him to get out and show it to Zoo-Zoo.

"All right," said the latter, glancing at it, "move on—" accompanying the remark with a jerk at the coat collar of the colored person, which sent him spinning several paces down the road.

"Now, sir, what do you want?" he said, addressing the astonished chivalry, who had by this time recovered his tongue, and replied:

"What? I want to go on, of course. That was my pass."

"Can't help it," replied Zoo-Zoo; "it says 'pass the bearer,' and the bearer of it has already passed. You can't get two men through this picket on one man's pass. That's so."

Chivalry reflected a moment, glanced at the bayonet before him, and then called out to his black man to come back. Sambo approached cautiously, but fell back in confusion, when the shooting-stick was brandished towards his own bosom.

"Where's your pass, sir?"

"Here, Massa," said the chattel, presenting the same one he had just received from his master in the carriage.

"Won't do," replied the holder of the bayonet. "That passes you to Fairfax. Can't let any one come from Fairfax on that ticket. Move on!" A stamp of the foot sent Sambo down the road at a hard gallop.

"Now, sir," he said, addressing the representative of F. F. V., "if you stay here any longer I'll tote you up to headquarters!"

Chivalry snatched his lines, wheeled around, and went off at the best trot his horses could make over the sacred soil, minus his chattel, who is still, probably, a free man.

SECESSION CRIMES.---A CURIOUS DOCUMENT.

A civil war is ever productive of heinous crimes—deeds that at other times would make the blood run cold, and would be too terrible to be repeated. The following plot to rob and murder seems almost too terrible, even for rebels.

Mr. Thomas West, an aged citizen of Lewis County, Ky., was found murdered a few steps from the house where he lived. At first it was thought that he was murdered for his money alone; but two days after the following strange document was found on

the promises of one not entirely above suspicion, which shows
that three others were to have been murdered that day for being
leading Union men; but Mr. West for the double crime of loyalty and having money. In looking over the circumstances
attending Major Hamrick, Captain Brewer, and 'Squire Evens,
on that memorable Sabbath day, it is pretty clear why they were
not killed; but to give particulars would require too much space.
The following is the paper found:

62	brack	must	be will		knows	nothing	bonds
26					that		
Jun	&	make	tom	at	boy	you	cesh
The	buck	arrangements		home	by	must	eternal
Funl	zol	to	sqr	by	send	do	in
comes	and	fix	for	him	I	sure	yours
off	you	sqr	place	self	certain	work	ours
and	place	and	good	be	meat	and	is
11 oc	hurs	old	a	shure	our	meet	field
mtz	on	tom	be	to	is	us	the
mag	house	dont	will	divide	cap	at	hell
H	tiggars	fail	walr	your	and	half	abes
cap	opposite	to	bear	animals	mag	breeds	to
B	ambs	secure	the	so	for	and	removed
will	be in	the	about	that	work	then	are
pass	will	last	there	you	shure	off	Your
up	me	for	from	can	make	for	these
to	and	our	come	dog	day	Dixey	
mtz	tigar	expense	must	then	all	if	

LION
TIGAR
ZOL
BUCK
BRACK

This paper is to be read down and up, and being interpreted
reads as follows:

1862, 26th of June.—The funeral comes off Sunday, 11 o'clock,
at Mount Zion. Major Hamrick and Captain Brewer will pass
up to Mount Zion. Tigar and I will be in ambush, opposite
Tigar's house, on the Hursh farm. You and Zol, Buck and
Brack, must make arrangements to fix 'Squire Evens and old
Thomas West. Do not fail to secure the last, for our expenses
must come from there. About the Bear Wallow will be a good
place for 'Squire. Thomas West will be at home by himself.
Be sure to divide your men so that you can watch them all day.
Make sure work; for Major and Captain are our meat certain.
I send by a boy that knows nothing. You must sure work,
and meet us at Half Breed's; and then off for D____ If these

four are removed to Abe's hell, the field is ours. Yours in
eternal Secesh bonds.

Signed by the following fictitious names: Lion, Tigar, Zol,
Buck, Brack.

ANECDOTE OF GOVERNOR TOD.

During the time that General Buckner and Staff were prisoners at Camp Chase, Governor Tod visited the camp, and was
received with "distinguished consideration." He was inducted
into the prisons, and in the Colonel's peculiarly pompous way,
introduced to the inmates. The first squad of prisoners to whom
the gubernatorial party paid their respects happened to be Gen.
Buckner's staff. "Governor Tod," said the Colonel. and the
Buckner party stood with hat in hand. The next party proved
to be a rough, uncouth band of guerrillas. The inevitable
"Governor Todd" was launched at them, and they, too, in their
awkward way, manifested their respect for the man who held in
his hand the power to release them from their captivity. The
Governor and Colonel proceeded on their way, followed by the
Buckners, meeting others, and paying and receiving their
respects, until a dark belt of contrabands loomed up in the
gubernatorial horizon. The darkies grinned at the distinguished
introduction, *and the distinguished Buckners made rapid tracks
for their quarters !* The Governor, who relishes fun, enjoyed
the scene hugely.

REVENGE INVERSELY.

A planter came into the camp of the 27th Illinois, at the Iuka,
and demanded two of his boys who had gone to work on the
fortifications. The Colonel refused to give them up, whereupon
the planter announced that he had a large plantation eighteen
miles off, with cotton and negroes, and money enough to support
a guerrilla band for a year, and he would do it, too, to be revenged for this wrong. He had hardly left camp, when one
hundred chosen men, with ten wagons, were dispatched for the
plantation, which reached their destination about midnight, and
by daylight fifty bales of cotton were in the wagons, and fifty-
three negroes, of all ages, shades and sexes, were in line with
all their duds, and the planter on horseback. This grand caval-
cade reached Iuka about three P. M. The planter was quartered

in the guard house, the male negroes on the fortifications, and
the women and children as cooks in the camp, and the cotton at
the depot, marked U. S. A few days, however, developed new
difficulties. The regiment had to move. The women could not
go along with ▓▓▓▓ babies, and the men did not want to go and
leave their ▓▓▓▓ The old planter was, however, sent North,
the men taken along, and most of the women and children sent
back to the plantation.

GENERAL BUTLER AND THE MAYOR OF NEW ORLEANS.

When General Butler took possession of New Orleans, the
conduct of the women (those who wear "purple and fine linen,"
and are popularly supposed to be ladies,) was disgusting, and
not calculated to strengthen one's faith in the possession of
common sense by the sex. Intrenching themselves behind the
immunities which the gallantry of our countrymen has ever
accorded them, they insulted and sneered at our officers and men
continually, and committed acts which would have insured six
months' hard labor at the forts to a man guilty of like actions.

General Butler soon after issued his famous order in regard
to women, which has been the subject of much comment, both
in the United States and Europe.

The Mayor became exceedingly angry, and addressed General
Butler a letter, in which he said:

"Your General Order is of a character so extraordinary, that
I can not suffer it to be promulgated, without protesting against
the threat it contains, which has already arroused the passions
of our people, and must exasperate them to a degree beyond
control."

He then went on to say that its phraseology was such that
officers and men could put the worst construction on it, and that
he did not anticipate a war on women and children.

To this General Butler replied:

"John L. Munroe, late Mayor of the city of New Orleans, is
relieved from all responsibility for the peace of the city, and is
suspended from the exercise of any official functions, and committed to Fort Jackson till further orders."

This brought the Mayor to the General's office in a hurry,
when, after an apology, the General agreed to let him off, allow-
ing him to publish the offensive letter and apology, and add that
the order applied only to those women who had insulted, by
word, look or gesture, the officers and soldiers of the United
States army.

The Mayor left, but afterward sent another letter, the counterpart of the first; and on the morning of the 19th of May, in company with several of his friends, including Judge Kennedy, John McClellan, Chief of Police, and D. G. Duncan, again demanded the right to witndraw his apology. The General, who had in view some treasonable acts of the Mayor, as well as his conduct in regard to the order, told him that he had played with the United States authority long enough, and must now go to Fort Jackson. His friends sharing in his opinions were dis-patched thither also.

HOW A REBEL WAS CONVERTED.

While Morgan was in Anderson county, one of his officers rode about twenty miles in advance of the command, in search of a good horse. Near Harrodsburgh he came to a house, in front of which he saw a blooded animal that just suited him. it belonged to a Mr. Nooks. The guerrilla dismounted and called upon the farmer. Mr. Nooks took him on sight for a Federal officer, and being himself a "vehement" rebel, was not at all pleased with the visit.

"Neighbor," said the officer, "I want something to eat; I'm hungry; let's have something good."

"Hain't got nuthin' to eat!" was the abrupt reply of the husbandman.

"Well, but I'm hungry—must have it. You don't want a man to starve here, do you?" said the Morganite.

"It's nuthin' to me. I don' care a d—n whether you starve or not. Nobody asked you to come here," quoth Mr. Nooks.

"You're so d—d saucy, I'll take your horse that's here, and leave you mine, while I go somewhere else for my dinner," said the soldier.

Mr. Nooks called one of his negroes to his assistance. The officer pulled a revolver, at the sight of which the darkey commenced a rapid retreat, and Mr. Nooks yielded a "tacit obedience." As the rebel mounted the thorough-bred, Mr. N. burst forth:

"Well, I hope to God Morgan will get after you. I don't care a d—n if he gets the horse;" to which the man on horseback retorted:

"Why, you old fool, I belong to Morgan's crowd," and rode off. Mr. Nooks has since been a consistent Union man. He says he didn't know Morgan was such a thief before.

DID NOT KNOW HOW TO RETREAT.

At the surrender of Munfordsville, Company K, of the 74th Indiana had been in the field such a short time that it knew little else than the manual of arms. The Major in command of the pickets of which Company K was a part, finding himself about to be surrounded, ordered a retreat; but Company K did not understand and remained in position fighting. The danger was imminent, and the Major who was commanding them had to go through the manual with Company K before it could be marched off. The company came to a shoulder arms! about face! forward! double-quick! march! and then left the field in good order!

"Boys," said a corporal, "I'm willing to stand treat any time, but this *retreat* don't suit me."

SINGULAR INCIDENT.

A young man, eighteen years of age, named Walker H. Henly, determined to join the rebel General Price's army, and accordingly started for the rebel camp. He had not traveled far, when he was overtaken and made prisoner by his father, who lost no time in bringing his rebellious son to St. Louis, and consigning him to the care of the Provost Marshal.

FEDERAL FERVOR.

The above is counterbalanced by the earnest devotion of a Union soldier, who, taking his leave to join the army, I said to him:

"Are you not afraid you will get killed?"

"No," said he. "When I made up my mind to go into the army, I offered my life in sacrifice to God and my country. I have given it up, and it matters not to me whether I die to-day or to-morrow; on the battle-field, in my tent, or in my bed; my life is my God's and my country's—no longer my own."

This is the spirit that prompted the brave sons of the North to strike for home and liberty.

THE ATMOSPHERE CREATED BY A BULLET.

The enemy were most splendidly armed with Enfield and Minnie rifles, throwing balls of English manufacture, with the box-wood plug in the base. The passage of these balls close to one's head, is followed by the most infernal hissing sound it is possible to imagine. Sometimes they seem to be endowed with vitality, and possessed of the most fiendish spirit of vindictiveness. Then again they remind you of geese following you in the road—not dangerous, but exasperating.

But the most singular thing is the effect of these balls upon the atmosphere through which they pass. The passage of one immediately across your face, is followed by a momentary sensation of deathly sickness. The air seems thick, stifling and putrid, like that of a newly-opened vault, accompanied by ar odor of certain kinds of fungi found in the woods.

LETTER FROM A COWARD.

Colonel Rodney Mason was accused of cowardice in surrendering his command at Clarksville, and when the affair was commented on in the Cincinnati Gazette, that paper received the following spicy epistle:

Mr. Editor:—I see in your paper of yesterday that you are trying to run down the 71st Regiment Ohio Volunteers now you lieing Devil if you don't quit publishing false hoods you had better. you was not with us at Shiloh ner at Clarksvill and how do you know? by your lieing inferments and that fellow who told you that the Rebils had no artillery and only three or four hundred men—is another licing whelp—— I think you had better turn out and go to war and see how brave you woul be —— ah! I you are to big a coward. you can stay at home and blab about those that have gone, you cowardly licing pup. dont say any thing more about the 71st now we haint all dead yet—

Col Mason done his duty at Shiloh and acted right at Clarksvill and he is a man, our boys all likes him and if he is dismissed from Service they will go to. col Mason is a brave man but disgraced for the deeds of which are praise worthy and you have no more sense than to run us down and publish us. now let the 71st rest. dont say any thing more about us. we have done our duty and are willing to do it still. but i would like to know if you are a union Man.

MAJOR WHALEY'S ADVENTURES.

Among the prisoners captured at Guyandotte was Major Whaley. It would be difficult to invent a piece of fiction to surpass, in the strangeness of its details, his escape from the rebels. The first day they marched forty miles, with nothing at all to eat. Many of the prisoners fainted, and Major Whaley begged his captors to take him and his comrades out into the woods and shoot them. The next day the rebels heard that Col. Zeigler had killed several secessionists in Guyandotte. This so enraged them that they rushed upon Whaley and his men, crying:

"Kill the d—d abolition cusses!"

But Col. Clark, who had some show of honor, interrupted.

"Shame on you, you cowardly whelps!" he exclaimed; "would you murder defenseless men? The first man who offers violence to these prisoners, it shall be the last of him. Do you hear? I'll cleave him in two!"

The men slunk away and attempted no further violence, though they took the opportunity, in the Colonel's absence, to heap upon the prisoners every indignity.

The next day they marched a distance of twenty miles. Here the cavalry separated and moved in different directions, leaving Major Whaley in charge of Captain Wicher. When night came, the Major, after hanging up his coat and hat by the fire to dry, went to bed in another room with Capt. Wicher. In this room there were eight men, one of whom acted as guard. About 3 o'clock, in the morning Whaley awoke, and finding the guard nodding in front of the fire, and all the rest in deep slumber, determined to effect his escape. Leaving his bed as quietly as possible, he approached the guard, and, ascertaining that he was asleep, secured Captain Wicher's hat, took his own shoes in his hand, and, seeing all clear outside, ran with all his might about two hundred yards down the Guyandotte river. Here he put on his shoes, and looked about for some drift wood upon which to cross the stream; but finding none, concluded to swim the river, which he did with considerable ease; but it was excessively cold, and his clothes nearly froze to him, and he was compelled to keep up a violent exercise to keep from being chilled to death. He then proceeded down the river about a mile and a half, and commenced to ascend a mountain, the summit of which he reached at daybreak, and just as Wicher was firing his guns as a signal of the escape. The firing was answered from all directions; Major Whaley, who knew it would be fatal to attempt to travel in daylight, sought a thicket of red oak brush, in which he found a sort of a path.

To and fro over this path he walked all day. A bleak wind was blowing, and being wet through, and having no coat, he was compelled to walk rapidly in order to save himself from perishing with cold.

When night came he started down the Guyandotte Valley, tracing the foot of the hills, a distance of two miles, when he

came upon a camp of about one hundred cavalry; and knowing
it would be folly to attempt to pass, retreated again to the moun-
tains. The next day he took a circuit upon the top of the hills,
to try and trace the valley and keep off the river, which he supposed would be guarded.

At last he came upon Hart's Creek, and, supposing himself to
be near a Union settlement, inquired of an old lady. One of
her sons offered to show him the way to Kyer's creek for two
dollars; and, when they started, another started also, and went
in another direction. The manner in which this was done excited the Major's suspicion. When they arrived at the creek, he
was not able to pay his guide, but he gave him all the money he
had—twenty-five cents—and a new pair of soldier's shoes, taking
in exchange the guide's old moccasins. The Major then hurried
down the creek as fast as possible, but had not gone far before
he heard the tramp of cavalry, and he had barely time to jump
a fence and secrete himself, before the horsemen dashed along
within six feet of where he lay, headed by the suspicious character before mentioned, but he escaped their observation.

The Major had now been three days without eating, and, discovering a house near by, he concluded he would venture the
consequences and go in. He had no arms, and did not deem it
safe to approach without them. Here was a dilemma; but food
he must have, and he felt that he might as well die in the attempt to get it, as to die for the want of it; so, taking a boulder
in each hand, he knocked at the door. Fortunately, the owner
was a Union man—like many others of the Western Virginia
stamp—and knew him at a glance. The Major told his case.

"I am sorry, Major," said the man, "that I can do nothing
for you. My neighbors are all rebels of the deepest dye, and,
if it should be known that I had helped a Lincolnite, myself
and family would be demolished instanter."

"But can't you give me something to eat, and a blanket?"
said the Major.

"There's a rebel, now!" said the man, and pointed to a rebel
soldier, who was approaching the house. "Here! quick! take
this blanket, slip out of the back door, and run for your life, and
don't let him see you."

The Major did as he was bid, and fortunately escaped without
being noticed; and he thus plodded on through a hot rebel region, skulking and hiding here and there, till, wearied and worn
out, he at last arrived safely at a Union camp.

REBEL VOLUNTEERS.

After the battle of Bull Run No. 2, a rebel soldier who had
received a frightful wound, was taken to the depot of Hooker's

wounded. While his wound was being dressed, he was asked if he owned any slaves.

"No," he answered.

"What, then, are you fighting for?"

"Well, I suppose we are fighting for those who do own them."

"What can it benefit you then?"

"It is no benefit to us sure, for these very men would kick us out of their houses, if we should attempt to equalize."

"O, that's very well for you to say, now that you are wounded and a prisoner; but what did you volunteer for?" said a bystander.

"Yes, I did volunteer; and who wouldn't? Who would want to wait to be drafted, and then be called a coward?"

"But you might not have been drafted."

"It's a slim chance of escape," replied the soldier. "They'll all have to go yet."

A-ZOUAVE JOKE.

A New York Zouave, in one of his scouting expeditions, captured a very fine horse. In a few days the owner came into camp and claimed the animal.

"The critter's confiscated," said Zoo-Zoo.

"But I'm not a rebel," said the man. "I'm Union, and the Government protects my property."

"Ya-as," drawled the Zouave, "I wouldn't give much for you loyal rebel's Union sentiment. It's too elastic."

"But I've taken the oath," persisted the man.

"Can't help if you have," replied Zoo-Zoo coolly, "the horse hain't, and I can't release him!"

The rebel never got his horse.

A SLAVE OFFERS A REWARD FOR HIS MASTER.

There was, in the Federal camp, a shrewd, witty darkie, who formerly belonged to a Wm. Duncan, of the rebel army. This negro could read and write, in fact, was a very well educated man. Some of the Kentuckians who had lost several slaves, had posted up around the encampment, "One hundred dollars reward. Ran away from the subscriber, my man Bob," etc.

Jim Duncan, as the boys called him, soon after issued the following, and placed it beside the other advertisements:

"50 CENTS REWARD.

"Ran away from dis chile, an' leff him all alone to take care of hisself after I done worked twenty-six years faithfully for him,

"MY MASSA, 'BILL DUNCAN.'

"Massa Bill is supposed to have done gone off wid de secesh-ers, for to *hunt for his rights*, and I speck he *done got lost.* Any pusson turnin' him to me, so dat he can take care of me—as he allers said 'Nigger' couldn't take care of hisself—will be much obliged to dis chile.

N. B.—Pussons huntin' for him please look in all de '*last ditches*,' as I often heerd him talk about goin' into de *diein'* business.   "Spectfully submitted,   JIM."

This "poster" created a great deal of merriment in camp, while the Kentucky residents who came across it, thought Jim a 'mighty sassy nigger."

LATE CONTRABAND NEWS.

When the United States vessels were on their way to attack Fernandina, they picked up a contraband who had ventured to sea in a small boat, to notify them that the rebels were deserting the place. While questioning the black, some of the officers of the Alabama remarked that he should have brought them news-papers to let them know what was going on.

"I thought of dat," replied the contraband, "and fotched a Charleston paper wid me."

With this he put his hand in his bosom and brought forth a paper, and, with the air of a man who was rendering an import-ant service, handed it to the circle of inquirers. They grasped it eagerly, but one glance induced a general burst of laughter, to the profound astonishment of poor Cuffee, who it seems could not read, and imagining that one paper was as good as another had brought one dated 1822. It is a little odd that this paper which has floated so long down the stream of time, contains an *article in favor of negro emancipation.*

A GOOD JOKE ON THE WAR POLICY.

During Pope's campaign in Virginia, the War Department one day sent to General Ripley, Chief of the Ordnance Department, for his estimate of the proper quantity of a certain kind of ammunition to be ordered. The General gave the figures, which were very large, and the messenger had reached the door to depart, when he called him back with "Of course you will double these estimates, as *we have to furnish both sides now.*"

KISSED THE WRONG CHAP.

A rebel soldier tells the following queer story :

Not long since a lot of us—I am H. P., high private now—were quartered in several wooden tenements, and in the inner room of one lay the *corpus* of a young secesh officer, awaiting burial.

The news soon spread to a village not far off. Down came tearing a sentimental, and not bad looking specimen of a Virginia dame.

"Let me kiss him for his mother!" she cried, as I interrupted her progress. "Do let me kiss him for his mother!"

"Kiss whom ?"

"The dear little lieutenant; the one who lies dead within. Point him out to me, sir, if you please. I never saw him, but—oh!"

I led her through a room in which a Union prisoner, a lieutenant, from Philadelphia, lay stretched out on an upturned trough fast asleep. Supposing him to be the "article" sought for, she rushed up, exclaiming: "Let me kiss him for his mother," approached her lips to his forehead. What was her amazement when the "corpse" ardently clasped its arms around her, returned the salute vigorously, and exclaimed:

"Never mind the old lady, Miss; go it on your own account. I havn't the slightest objection."

ADVENTURES OF A REBEL EMISSARY.

One day a man, dressed in well-worn working clothes, presented himself to the United States Provost Marshal on the United States side of the Suspension Bridge. He wore a pair of very short trousers of striped Kentucky jean, and a seedy coat of the same material. A coarse, not over-clean shirt, and a jagged straw hat, completed the costume. The man had no collar nor cravat, and his face was apparently greatly tanned by exposure to the weather.

He wanted to go over the river, he said, but had no pass and did not know that any would be needed. He stated that he was an Englishman from Cornwall, and a miner by trade. He had been working for some time in Pennsylvania, but had lately received a letter from his brother, a farmer near London, Canada West, stating that he was short of help, and requesting his miner relative to come on to his assistance, at least till the harvest time was over.

The miner held his tools in one hand, and in the other carried an old carpet bag of the black glazed style in common use. The glazing, in many places, was come off, and the outside was, moreover, spotted and soiled with dirt.

This carpet bag was more valuable than the famous one of John Brown; for it contained the papers, dispatches and money of the rebel emissary Sanders.

The Marshal pondered a while, but the poor miner gave such a consistent story, and seemed so disappointed at his unexpected trouble in crossing, that the official's heart was melted, and he gave him the required pass.

The toll-man of the Suspension Bridge then demanded a quarter of a dollar toll.

"Two shillings," said the miner, "why, I can't give it. I've only got one shilling."

The plea of poverty completely disarmed whatever shadow of suspicion may have existed in regard to the poor workman; after the proper degree of hesitation, the "fellow" was allowed to pass over at half price.

Thanking the toll keeper for his liberality, the miner walked on wearily across the bridge. As he neared the Canada side his step became lighter—just as Christian (pardon the comparison) felt when the burden dropped off his back. A decided burden had dropped off of George N. Sanders' mind—he was safe in Canada.

Arriving at the Canada side of the bridge, the miner, with his tools and carpet-bag, jumped into the Clifton House omnibus and was quickly driven to that hotel. He went to the desk and registered on the book the initials S. N. G., his own initials reversed.

The clerk looked at the shabby working man a moment, and then coldly said:

"We can't give you a room here, sir."

"But I must have a room," said Sanders.

"None to spare to-night," replied the clerk.

The miner thrust his hand in his pocket and drew forth a great roll of "green-backs."

"Here," said he to the clerk, "take these as security. Put them in your safe; but give me a room at once."

Of course money has its effect in Clifton House, as everywhere else. Still the clerk hesitated.

"Is there any place about here where I can get a respectable
suit of clothes?" asked the miner, dropping his Cornish dialect.

There was no place nearer than the bridge, a mile distant; so
the miner again insisted on having the room, and, as it was obvious that "things were not as they seem," he was shown to a
suitable apartment.

A few minutes afterwards a guest strolled out on the piazza,
where ex-Governor Morehead, of Kentucky, was sitting.

"By the way, Governor," said he, "what a singular old fellow that was in the office. He registered his name on the book
only in initials."

"Good God! in initials!" cried Morehead, starting up; "he's
come then;" and, rushing past the astonished guest, he demanded
to be shown to the room of the mysterious S. N. G.

Other secessionists also hastened thither. Sanders was pro-
vided with a suit of clothes at once; the clerks and servants al-
tered their deportment to the quondam miner, and the guests
had a rare piece of gossip to talk about. Sanders' trick was
a capital success; and, whatever is thought of him or his cause,
it is generally acknowledged that his journey from Richmond to
Canada is one of the "cutest" specimens of rebel 'strategy" the
war has produced. It shows that our blockade is so stringent
that a rebel emissary prefers a long land journey in disguise to
attempting to break it.

Of course, the adventure was the chief topic of gossip in the
Niagara hotels; and miners will henceforth be viewed with a
very profound suspicion in the neighborhood of the Suspension
Bridge.

A COMICAL MUSIC BAND.

A very amusing anecdote is told of the Cumberland Gap army
on its retreat through Kentucky, which deserves to stand beside
Lever's story of Major O'Shaughnessy and the Duke of Welling-
ton.

After the army had been out from the Gap three or four days,
it was found utterly impossible to subsist the men without foraging, and in consequence the country along the road was laid
under contribution for all the eatables that could be found. Of
course everything was paid for as far as possible, but the necessity of letting each soldier be his own commissary made sad
havoc with discipline for the time. One morning, after the boys
in DeCourcey's brigade had been foraging about with such success that nearly every one had a chicken, duck, goose or pig in
his hand, they approached a considerable town, through which

the commander desired them to pass in as imposing a manner as possible. He ordered the band to the head of the column, arms to the "shoulder," the easy route step changed to the prim parade step, and got all ready for an impressive military display. But the boys didn't fancy being put on their good behavior with such dirty old rags as they had on, and determined that they as well as the colonel would have their fun out of the thing. So, when the band struck up "Hail Columbia," and the notes came echoing down the line, the colonel's ears were astonished with a horrible chorus of squawks, squeaks and cackles, enough to drown the roar of a twelve pounder. Every man had turned his duck, pig or chicken into a private concert for his own enjoyment, by means of judicious pinches and punches, and, as far as the ear could hear, the uproar of a thousand barnyards broke loose, swelled up as the companies came along. Such another parade was never seen on the face of the earth before. The colonel relished the joke exceedingly, and suffered the concert to continue till they were well out of the town.

WOULDN'T RESIGN.

A Rev. Mr. Brush was appointed Colonel of the 38th Iowa. His unpopularity with his men was so great, that Governor Kirkwood visited Dubuque to persuade him to resign.

Colonel Brush, with all the line officers, came trooping down to the hotel, and were immediately favored with an audience by the Governor.

Every line officer, with the utmost solemnity, protested that he did not desire to serve under Brush in any form; that none of them had any confidence in him, and that he should, in honor —having thus lost the respect of all his officers—resign. This they said, ranged in line, and confronting the Colonel.

The Colonel declared, in response, that the whole trouble arose out of the fact, that he declined to appoint the brother of Postmaster David, Adjutant of his Regiment, and on account of some difficulty in the selection of Sutler. That, and only that, was the occasion of the feeling. The following colloquy then took place:

Governor.—I do not see, Colonel, with such a feeling existing, how you can, with pleasure or profit, hold your present position. I would advise you to resign.

Col. Brush.—When there shall be proper charges brought against me in the manner specified, I will, if found guilty, suffer the penalty, but shall not resign.

5

Governor.—But these men declare you are inexperienced and incompetent.

Col. Brush.—If that is an objection of so grave a nature, it is one which would lead almost every Iowa officer to resign. I am not the only Colonel you have appointed, Governor, who is inexperienced, and may be incompetent.

Governor.—Well, Colonel, I had rather trundle a wheelbarrow for a living than hold your position under the circumstances.

Col. Brush.—Very likely, Governor, but I had rather be Colonel.

Governor.—Then you refuse to resign?

Col. Brush.—Yes. If you have any way you can deprive me of my commission, and desire to do so, why, do it, that is all; but I fail to find any process by which such a case can be reached, except by a court-martial. Of course, I am open to that.

Governor.—Well, it is of no use, gentlemen.

Upon which all took their leave. It was a rich scene: the Governor a little excited, the Colonel as cool and imperturbable as an eight day clock.

A SAD BLUNDER.

Military commanders have been guilty of many blunders, and this is one of them:

During the battles on the Potomac, the 3rd Michigan went into the battle with two hundred and ninety men, and came out with only one hundred and forty-six, and more than three-fourths of this number met their fate by the fire of the 20th Indiana regiment, which lapped over their rear and poured a galling fire into them while on the advance. The first knowledge which the Michigan boys had of the presence of the other regiment, was the bullets in the back of their heads, arms, etc., nearly half of the regiment having lapped across them.

Sad must be the sorrow of those whose friends fall—not in their country's cause—but through the carelessness of her commanders.

CLOSE SHOOTING.

At the battle of Fair Oaks the enemy posted a number of sharpshooters in trees, and when the Excelsior Brigade drove off the rebels at the point of the bayonet, some of these fellows were left. One of them was espied by one of the Excelsiors, and as the discovery was mutual, each drew sight on his opponent. The rebel fired first, his bullet whizzing in close proximity to the Union soldier, and then dropping his gun, exclaimed: "Hold on! I surrender."

He spoke too late. The deliberate musket of the Yankee was pointing death at the trembling rebel. The trigger was already pulled, and the next instant a minnie ball crashed through his brain, and he fell through the branches a mangled corpse. Said one of our wounded who was lying near at the time and described the scene:

"It was terrible to see him drop."

HAIR BREADTH ESCAPES.

At the battle of Antietam, a Vermont soldier got strayed away from his regiment, and finding it impossible to return, concluded to fight on his own hook. Happening to see a hollow stump, he got inside, and in that position fired ninety shots, part of which he gathered from the dead soldiers around him. During this time the balls whistled about his fortification, as he described it, "like a nor' wester round a log barn," several of them striking the stump. At last a shell exploded over his head, a piece of which fell inside the stump. Thinking it rather hot he evacuated his fort, and before he had gone ten steps another shell fell in the very spot he had left, tearing the stamp into shivers.

One of the Texas soldiers was advancing with his bayonet upon a Lieutenant of the 9th Iowa, whose sword had been broken. The officer saw his intention, avoided the thrust, fell down at his foeman's feet, caught hold of his legs, threw him heavily to the ground, and before he could rise drew a long knife from his adversary's belt and buried it in his bosom.

The Texan, with dying grasp, seized the Lieutenant by the hair, and sank down lifeless, bathing the brown leaves with his blood. So firm was the hold of the nerveless hand, that it was necessary to cut the hair from the head of the officer before he could be freed from the corpse of his foe.

Among the phenomena of the fight was the condition of the uniform of Captain Bennett. It had eight bullet holes in it. One through the collar of his coat, one through the right coat sleeve, one through his pantaloons below the left knee, one through both pantaloons and drawers above the right knee, and through the skirts of his coat. There was not a scratch on this man's skin.

A soldier came suddenly upon a number of the enemy, who fired at him. Suddenly retreating, his knapsack, belt, indeed his entire "traps," were shot away, but he got off without a wound.

Corporal Springer, of the 13th Indiana, whom Colonel Wilder says is the best soldier he ever saw in danger, had charge of the rifled gun near the stockade. He would jump on the parapet to see the effect of his shots, amidst a hail storm of balls. He saw Bragg and Buckner and staffs, riding a mile distant, and fired at them. Buckner afterward inquired after Springer, and stated that the first of his two shells struck within thirty feet, and the second passed within four feet of his head without exploding.

At Mountain Run, a small branch which joins the Rappahannock, a Federal battery of six pieces commenced to throw shells by way of diversion, but were promptly engaged by the Donaldsonville battery (Louisiana), Capt. Mora, and soon after retired. In this affair General Roger A. Pryor had a narrow escape. While sitting on a fence by the roadside, a shell burst immediately over his head, and the fragments dashed into the ground around him on every side, without doing injury.

"Humph," said Pryor, "they mistake my position. I am not so *high* as that."

He wore a high felt hat, and was in plain sight of the Federal artillerists, who were probably amusing themselves by firing at so important a target.

General Wilcox likewise received similar attentions. He was riding in advance of the army, attended by a single trooper, when the latter discovered one of the Yankee pickets peeping over the top of a boulder.

"Shall I bring him down?" said the soldier, raising his piece to his shoulder.

"No," replied the General; "the distance is too great; better not waste your powder."

Hardly were the words out of his mouth before "whiz"—a Minnie ball flew within three inches of the General's ear, and lodged in the bank behind him.

"You may shoot," said Wilcox.

While the division of General Kearney was halting at Manassas Junction, General Kearney suggested to Brigadier General Birney the propriety of making a reconnoissance towards Centerville. General Birney took with him some two or three orderlies, and about twenty cavalrymen, and started in the direction indicated, to which point, from Manassas, the distance is four miles. As he proceeded along he saw nothing of Secesh, but as a precautionary measure, and to prevent surprise, he would occasionally send one of the cavalry in this direction, another in some other, and by so doing lessening the number he had with him to such an extent that when he reached Centerville he had but two orderlies and four cavalrymen.

As they rode into the town it appeared deserted, and they commenced making preparations for a comfortable and permanent stay. While halting in front of the only tavern in the place, one of his orderlies rode up to him and stated that there were then coming up the hill a body of our own cavalrymen, having with them the Stars and Stripes.

The General was about to go and meet them, when remembering that it was hardly possible for any of our troops to approach from that direction, he determined to make an observation before proceeding further. Hardly had he came to this determination, when the body of troops spoken of reached the brow of the hill. They, discovering that they were so near a Union General, gave one of their peculiar yells, and rushed toward him. His party, seeing the trap they were in, put spurs to their horses, and started on a full gallop towards their own encampment. hotly pursued by the rebels.

This was kept up until just across Bull Run, when the Colonel of the rebels, who was mounted on a splendid horse, came so near the General as to draw his sword upon him, but when in the act of raising to strike, General Birney suddenly turned, and with his pistol shot the Colonel in the region of the heart.

At this point the General had stationed a regiment, to do duty as pickets.. They, previously hearing the commotion, were drawn up in line. The General immediately rode to the rear, giving the order to fire, which they did promptly, thus checking the pursuit of the rebels, killing some twenty, and taking quite a number prisoners.

These troops were all attired in the uniform of Uncle Sam, and had with them the Stars and Stripes. A conversation had with the wounded Colonel before he died, disclosed the fact that in this uniform and with these colors, they had frequently been within our lines, and that it was their intention to visit Washington at some future time in the same disguise.

General Birney was much complimented upon the cool daring displayed upon this occasion.

Lieutenant Colonel Herron, of the 9th Iowa, was surrounded by ten or twelve of the enemy, and ordered to surrender. He indignantly refused, and with his revolver in one hand, and his sword in the other, kept his enemies at bay, by placing his back against a tree. He had killed and wounded four of the rebels, when, having been twice wounded himself, his sword was knocked from his grasp, and his arms seized from behind. He would have been killed, had not a southern Captain, from admiration of his courage, ordered his life to be spared. Even while the

Colonel was a captive, a Creek Indian stole up, and was about to plunge a knife into his side, when the Captain drew his revolver and blew out the treacherous creature's brains.

A printer from Indiana, a perfectly raw recruit, sat at an embrasure and fired over five hundred shots. He kept up all the time a continuous laugh in the ranks about him, by his witty and humorous remarks. The men below loaded for him, and he fired rapidly and with splendid effect.

"Right in the mouth," he would exclaim, after an effective shot; "There's a job for the Dentist. Give us another gun."

He managed to escape without being parolled.

A brave little fellow, of not more than seventeen, belonging to the 9th New York, stood in front of his regiment while it engaged the enemy, at short range, in which position he fired all his cartridges, and, stooping down, took his dead comrade's cartridge box and fired the entire contents, in all ninety-five rounds, not receiving a scratch the whole time, notwithstanding the ground was covered with the dead and wounded all around him. The regiment was ordered to charge a rifle-pit, where the rebels were concealed, and the young hero was the first who entered it, the enemy flying at the approach of the bayonet.

Among the most cool and fearless of the Indiana officers is General R. S. Foster. When he arrived at Winchester, with his command, they were plodding along under "right shoulder shift," and the General, not deeming this rebellious city worthy any respect, did not bring the boys to "shoulder," nor change the easy, sauntering tramp of the march to the trim step of parade. When they had got fairly into the city, they were saluted with sundry volleys of rebel musketry, which were repeated till they were "past the outmost guards" of the town. The bullets whistled past their ears, and clattered against their bayonets, but not a man looked around, nor swerved to the right or left. The General rode on, and the men followed, as though nothing had happened. Not a man was hurt.

At another time, when Foster was Colonel of the 13th Indiana, and when he was marching his regiment into Phillippi, finding the boys pretty loose, and straggling along without much order, he sung out:

"Close up, boys! close up! If the rebels should fire on you, scattered as you are, they wouldn't hit a d—d one of you!"

The boys, relishing the joke exceedingly, and not desiring to be considered so poor a mark, closed up immediately.

A member of the 11th Indiana, while out scouting, was fired upon by a squad of rebels: and, as they approached him, he fell flat upon his face in the mud.

"Now we've got you!" exclaimed the rebels, rushing upon him.

"No you hain't!" returned the Hoosier, springing to his feet; and, placing his thumb to his nose, he continued:

"You can't come it." And, while his would-be captors were recovering from their astonishment, he turned and run. The bullets from a score of muskets followed him, but he escaped unhurt.

A private, who was standing near General Roseerans, noticed a rebel who was raising his gun, and appeared to be endeavoring to get a good aim on the General. The private immediately rested his gun over the rump of his commander's horse, and brought the rebel down. Both guns went off at the same time, but the rebel bullet went high above its mark.

As an Indiana soldier was passing through a piece of woods, he saw a couple of rebels with a wagon, toiling along through a swamp near by. When they saw him they hailed him:

"Helloa, stranger, we're out of water; wouldn't you give us a drink from your canteen?"

The soldier stepped up and gave them the drink, and started again on his march; but he had not got ten paces before he heard an ominous "click." He turned around, and saw one of the rebels drawing a bead on him. The trigger was pulled and the cap exploded, but the gun did not go off. He immediately raised his gun, and ordered them to move on with their team, which they did, in the direction which he told them. So the brave Hoosier walked behind, with his ready gun leveled upon them, till he had them safely into camp, and delivered up as prisoners of war.

HUMORS OF THE DRAFT.

When it was fully realized that a slight draft was to be made throughout the North, an epidemic inability followed in the wake of this paralyzing idea; old diseases were brought into requisition, and new ones spontaneously sprung into existence. The class of people, however, who seemed predisposed to this disease, to the honor of the Union be it said, were those who were opposed to the war, with, perhaps, a slight sprinkling of cowards, and a few sporadic cases of "conscientious scruples." To these few, then, and not to the many who freely marched into the ranks, at the call of the draft, do these remarks apply.

One of the most remarkable cases of exemption was that of a merchant in a lucrative business, who cut off the fore-finger of his right hand, and when he was afterwards reproached for it, and denounced as a coward, replied :

"Well, my wife was afraid I should be drafted, and so, when I was asleep, she cut off my finger, and I knew nothing about it."

"It is strange you should not know it," said one.

"It's a fact though," he replied innocently, "when I woke up she had it off and all tied up."

Astonishing as was this performance, it did not satisfy the loyal citizens, for they stretched a line across the street in front of his store, hung upon it a huge banner, on which was written: "Coward," and other words expressing their indignation.

He was then ordered to leave the town, which he did.

Another, a huge able-bodied fellow, came before the Examiners with a "bran new truss." Upon being ordered to take it off, he said pitifully:

"Indeed, I dare not do it; my whole insides will all come out!"

The surgeon, however, removed the truss, when, to the astonishment of all, the concealed part was as smooth and perfect as the rest of his hide.

"You'll do to fight," said the surgeon, and the fellow backed out amid the hearty laughter of the crowd.

A stout, able-bodied man, whose brawny arms and spatula fingers looked as though they might be able to wield the sledge of Vulcan, came before the board, and confidently held up his right hand, which was minus the fore finger. The stump, however, was scarcely healed over, and the deputy assured the board that, when he was enrolled, he had all his fingers on.

"But I accidentally cut one off since," replied the man, earnestly.

A witness was then brought forward who testified that he saw the man deliberately, and not accidentally, cut off one half of his finger, and that he said, when he had done so, that it was a good joke on the draft, as that would exempt him. He was not exempted.

A drafted man, who had been in camp about two weeks, got a furlough to visit his sweetheart. After sitting up with her to an extremely reasonable hour, and talking over what she imagined his unlucky fate, and their future prospects, his lady-love prevailed upon him to lie down and get one more good sleep; and accordingly, when her patriotic lover began to snore freely, she conceived the happy idea of exempting him from the draft. She would rather lose his finger than his whole body, so, taking an axe, and carefully laying the finger on a block, with one blow she severed it from the hand and him from the army. The operation of course awoke him, when he upbraided her for her cruelty and want of patriotism, and reported himself at camp, remarking:

"No woman, however sweet, is going to prevent me from serving my country when called to do so. I have lost my finger, but she has lost her lover."

A very conscientious gentleman attended the lottery drawings at the Court House, and after looking on a while, he approached the Commissioner and said :

"I say, 'Squire, can't you find some other way to choose drafted men than by gambling in that style?"

"No, sir. It is the fairest way in the world. There can be no cheating."

"It's gambling, nevertheless, and as I've got conscientious scruples about engaging in games of chance, I want you to take my name out of that box."

The Commissioner informed the over-scrupulous gentleman that it was too late in the day to accept such a plea. The lottery business went on, and fortunately for him, the opponent to gambling drew a blank.

In a towhship where secession predominated, a heavy draft was to be made from its active militia. To satisfy those who were disposed to grumble, and to give them no opportunity to misrepresent matters, the Draft Commissioner invited them to send a committee to the Court House to witness the drawing. They accepted the invitation, appointing on the committee some of the deepest-dyed Butternuts of the township. One of the leaders was asked to shake the box. He shook it, and in so doing accepted the apothecary's motto: "When taken to be well shaken." He shook the box well, and the blind-folded draftsman drew therefrom the name of the old fellow's son. This rather disconcerted him, but he resolved to shake the box before the next name should be drawn. This time he shook it worse than before, and the unlucky ballot which followed the shaking had upon it his son-in-law's name. Thinking this too much of a good thing, he turned on his heel and left the Court House, remarking:

"I'm blowed if I have any thing more to do with this gambling institution."

A Lieutenant in a volunteer regiment sold himself as a substitute, and was accepted. The officer supposed that he could still retain his office, and he chuckled at the idea of making a few hundred clear profit so easily, but was exceedingly astonished when he woke up to the stern fact that he had lost his commission, and was compelled to serve as a private.

Another gentleman, who had been a Major General in the Militia, when he was drafted, reported himself at headquarters with his regimentals on, ready for duty, to take the command of any division that should be assigned him; but he was exceedingly shocked and astonished when informed that they were not drafting Major Generals, and that he was only a private.

THE HANDWRITING ON THE WALL.

Some Southern gentleman, whose sympathies are seen in his writing, amused himself one night by writing on the outer walls of some of the prominent houses in Richmond. The chivalrous inhabitants were astonished the next morning when they read the following mottoes:

"On Yorktown's walls the cry is 'still they come.'"

"Change your bells into cannon, and charge with Confederate 5's."

"Southern Legions covered with glory: 'Pinks of chivalry.'"

"The Lord is on our side, but in consequence of pressing engagements elsewhere, could not attend at Pea Ridge, Donelson, &c., &c."

"He will also be prevented from visiting his chosen 'pinks' at Yorktown."

"Southern hearts are beating low—
Manassas boasters shun the foe;
Stars and Stripes shall wave again—
Northerners tread this ebon main."

"Something new under the sun, to-wit: 'Petticoat gunboats.'"

"Nationals! unfurl your banners over Yorktown walls."

"Southern boasters, grasp the dust,
In the Lord you vainly trust.
For the Lord you fain would cheat
With Halcyon lips and Pluto's feet."

"The cry is still they come."

"Hang your banners on the outer walls."

Had this loyal gentleman been discovered, he would probably have been hung on the outer walls himself.

TAKING THE OATH.

When Cox's brigade entered a small town in Virginia, it produced a terrible scare among the inhabitants. They hid in the

cellars, cupboards, and in every hole where they felt that they
would be safe from the barbarous hands of these vandal Yankees. One little girl buried herself under the bed clothes, at
the risk of suffocation, evidently endeavoring to smother her own
screams.

Lieut. Krin, of General Pleasanton's staff, who was appointed
Provost Marshal of the village, immediately arrested all the male
citizens of the place, and assembled them in front of one of the
stores, preparatory to taking the oath. Twenty-six comprised
the number, consisting of old men, middle-aged, and youths.
They answered as their names were called.

"I don't like to take this oath of allegiance on Southern soil.
It's shameful!" said a plethoric Methodist clergyman.

"I think you are rather premature," said an old man of sev-
enty. "to force this upon us before we have had time to think
of it."

"You will soon be gone, and then the Confederates will come
in and play the devil with us, if we take the oath," said a Virginia rough.

So, one after another offered his excuse for not being loyal.
But these excuses proved of no avail. As fast as their names
were called off, and their refusal heard, a significant dash of the
pen confiscated their homes, and awarded them confinement.

"*No, sir!*" replied Richard Wilmot, in an insolent and defiant
manner. This answer probably prolonged his time in the prison.
Not one of them subscribed to the oath.

A LUDICROUS SCENE.

While the Union troops occupied Phillippi, Colonel Crittenden
one day took his regiment out about a mile, to an open place, for
the purpose of giving them a little practice. This move was
without orders, and consequently, when the firing was heard, all
supposed that the rebels were upon them. Immediately the
whole camp was astir, and soon in battle array.

At this time General Dumont, who was then Colonel, was lying
sick upon his couch, and although convalescent, was quite too
feeble to walk without help. Hearing the confusion without, he
inquired the cause, and upon being told, he sprang out of bed
and attempted to put on his clothes, but before he was half
dressed he fell back upon his couch exhausted. Dr. Thompson,
the surgeon in charge, and the special friend of the General,
endeavored to dissuade him from so rash an act.

"It can't be helped," replied the General, "I must be with my
regiment."

· So, between alternate dressing and resting, he was at last all
rigged *cap-a-pie*, for the coming battle. His horse was brought,
and the surgeon helped him on, but he was too weak to sit there
steadily, and it was with some difficulty that he could retain his
seat in the saddle. At last his regiment was in line of battle.
The General cast his eye down the line with some pride, and
then straightening himself in his stirrups, while he swayed to
and fro from weakness, in a slow, measured voice said :
      "Now let the —— rebels come on. I'm ready for them."
      The General is in health small and thin, and was on this occa-
sion much smaller and thinner than usual ; but his language
and attitude were so ludicrously at variance, that his staff, and
the surgeon, who were present, could not resist the impulse to
indulge in a gentle laugh. Yet they knew that the soldier's
heart burned in his bosom, and were convinced that he felt that
he could do double duty did the occasion require it.
      Presently an orderly rode up at full gallop and reported :
      " A false alarm. The firing is from Colonel Crittenden's regi-
ment, who are out practicing."
      "Ah, practicing," said the General. "He thinks he can't do
us any good, so he goes out to shoot at nothing."
· This remark was well understood by his hearers, who considered it a good joke.

RECKLESS DARING.

All wars have developed those fearless characters who have
no realization of death and danger; but this rebellion has the
honor, if honor it be, of producing more men of this reckless
stamp than any war in all the annals of history. There are
many soldiers, in both armies, who have carried their bravery
to sheer recklessness, and many a life has thus been sacrificed
to their extravagant daring.
      At the battle of Antietam, the national flag of the 30th Ohio
came out with seventeen bullet holes through it. This regiment,
from its advanced position, received the rebel fire from two sides,
and at last was forced to fall back, when the brave color-bearer,
sergeant White, recklessly planted the flag in the very face of
the foe. The rebels rewarded his daring by firing a volley upon
him, killing him instantly. Another soldier caught the flag, and
amid the whistling bullets, bore it triumphantly away.
      A rebel flag was borne seven times to the fort, on the acute
angle of the left line of fortifications, and was seven times shot
away. The last attempt to plant it there was made by a daring

fellow who received twenty-seven shots through the body before
he fell.

The force under General Sigel was gallantly charging the
enemy and driving them from the heights they occupied, when
a rebel officer, Captain of a Louisiana company, seemed resolved
to throw away his life. As his fellow-soldiers retreated, he advanced further toward our troops, until he was almost alone.
He waved his sword and cried in a loud, ringing voice, for his
men to follow him, and denouncing them as cowards if they
retreated. They heeded not his appeals; and seeing himself
deserted, he ran toward our advance shouting like a madman:
"I am as brave as Cæsar. If we are whipped I do not want
to live. Come on you d—d Yankees."

Our infantry were anxious to take this southern Hotspur prisoner, and would have done so had not one of our batteries
opened from the left on the retreating foe, and in its storm of
iron swept down the single life, which, so full of fierceness, ebbed
itself away in the sodden and unpitying ground.

After the battle, inquiries were made of some of the Louisiana
prisoners concerning the fallen Captain. No one knew his name,
but several said they believed he was the son of a sugar planter
living up the Bayou La Fourche, who had joined the southern
army because he said he wanted to die; that if not killed before
the war was over, he would commit suicide. That some secret
sorrow or remorse tortured him night and day, there was no
reason to doubt. He was often gentle, generous, and affectionate,
but under the influence of liquor, which he drank to excess,
overbearing, rude and violent. He had fought two duels in Ar-
kansas with his fellow-officers, and had thrice been attacked with
the delirium tremens, that familiar foe to southern youth and
southern age. Doubtless, on the morning when he so wantonly
sacrified himself, liquor had turned his brain, and he found the
death, he sought so perseveringly, amid the iron tempest of de-
structive battle.

James Hartley, who had lost a brother, swore to be revenged,
and in one of the sorties by the rebels, attacked six of them
single handed, and killed three before he lost his own life.

Three members of the 8th Illinois rushed over the rifle pits,
after the enemy had retreated, and frantically hurled themselves
into the midst of a thousand foes. They never returned.

At the battle of Shiloh, Brigadier General Gladden, of South
Carolina, who was in General Bragg's command, had his left arm
shattered by a ball on the first day of the fight. Amputation
was performed hastily by his staff-surgeon on the field; and then,
instead of being taken to the rear for quiet and nursing, he

mounted his horse, against the most earnest remonstrances of all his staff, and continued to command. The next day he was again in the saddle, and kept it during the day; on the next, he rode on horseback to Corinth, twenty miles from the scene of action, and continued to discharge the duties of an officer. In a few days, a second amputation, near the shoulder, was necessary, when General Bragg sent an aid to ask if he would not be relieved of his command, to which he replied:

"Give General Bragg my compliments, and say that General Gladden will only give up his command to go into his coffin."

Against the remonstrances of personal friends, and the positive injunctions of the surgeons, he persisted in sitting up in his chair, receiving dispatches and giving directions, till the next day, when lockjaw seized him, and he died in a few moments.

A rebel private left his company, and, clubbing his gun, rushed into a Union regiment, and aimed a blow at an Indiana captain, who dodged the blow and shot the rebel.

A rebel officer, after all his companions had retreated and left him, fought with his sword against a half dozen Unionists, who had surrounded him, and were anxious to take him prisoner.

"Do you surrender?" asked a Union soldier.

"Never!" exclaimed the rebel defiantly, while his sword hissed through the air in defiant curves.

Three of the Union soldiers were wounded, yet they wished to save him on account of his bravery, and again one of them cried:

"Will you surrender?"

"I'll die first!" was his answer, and with the word came a blow that carried death to a Union soldier. Instantly a bayonet put an end to his brief but brave career.

Another soldier mounted the breastworks in full view of the Federal forces, and shouted:

"Come on, you cussed cowardly Yankees! Shoot away, you thieving pups! Who cares for your bullets? I'm bullet-proof!"

The defiance was scarcely uttered before he fell, pierced by a score of the bullets he held in such contempt.

A soldier from Rhode Island, while on picket guard, was rushed upon by a party of rebel cavalry. He instantly fired his piece at the foremost, and ran. The way before him was an open field, about fifty rods across, the other side being hemmed in by an old, rotten log fence, and, still beyond, a sort of chaparral of briar bushes and underbrush. To this retreat the soldier started, on quadruple quick, with a half dozen horsemen after him. Fortunately for the soldier, the rains had made the field quite muddy, and the horses slumped through the turf so badly that they could not lessen the distance between them and the fugitive.

All this time the rebels were keeping up a roar of *pistolry*, one
of the balls passing through the soldier's hat, and another went
clean through his cartridge box and lodged in his coat. Still on
ran the hero, and still on splashed the horsemen. The picket
at last reached the fence, and with one bound landed on the top,
intending to give a long spring ahead; but the fence was frail,
and crumbled beneath his weight. It so chanced that a hog had
rooted out a gutter at this place, and was lying snoring therein.
At the cracking of the fence, his swineship evacuated his hole,
and scampered, barking, into the underbrush. As luck would
have it, the soldier fell in that hole, muddy as it was, and the
fence rattled down upon him. This was no more than fairly
done when up came the horsemen, and, hearing the rustling of
leaves, and not doubting it was their prey, dashed through the
gap in the fence, and, seeing a path in the brush, they put through
it after the hog, and were soon out of sight. When the sound
of their footsteps died away, the picket returned to camp and
reported. The next day one of these rebel horsemen was taken
prisoner. When our hero saw him he recognized him at once,
and sung out:

"I say, old fellow, did you catch that hog yesterday?"

"We did that," retorted the prisoner, "but it wasn't the one
we were after."

LOVE AND GLORY.

At the battle of Donelson a prisoner, who had received a
mortal wound, told the following sad story:

I am a native of Pennsylvania. Several years ago I removed
to Tennessee. While there I became acquainted with a Southern lady. She was a high spirited girl; intelligent, of good
education, wealthy, and moved in the highest circles of society.
I loved her and sought her hand. We were plighted, and our
nuptials were about to take place when the war broke out. At
heart I felt the enormity of this wicked rebellion, but knowing
the peculiar southern proclivities of my affianced, and her bitter
hatred of the North, I almost dreaded to meet her, and when we
did meet it proved as I expected. She was a rank rebel.

"What is to be done, Delia?" said I, after a long conversation.
"Our views do not harmonize in this matter."

"What do you intend to do?" she asked.

"Nothing," replied I, with some misgiving. "I can never lift
my hand against the best Government the world has ever produced; neither can I turn against the people of the South, whom
I so respect, and who are the kinsmen of my Delia. I must be

non est in this matter, and leave more belligerent ones to do the fighting."

Tenderly as I said this, I noticed that she was agitated, and her eyes almost flashed fire as she answered:

"But you *must* do something."

"What *can* I do, Delia, under such peculiar circumstances?" said I.

"Can't you fight for the country that protects you? The glorious South, that gives you wealth, love and happiness?" she said, earnestly.

"Would you have me turn traitor, and destroy the very government that has given me all these?" said I.

"Traitor!" she exclaimed, wildly, "Is he a traitor who fights for her he loves? Traitor, indeed! Can you not fight for *me*, William? Then you are a traitor in the worst sense of the word."

I was nettled, and my face showed it; but love conquers every thing, even loyalty, and I said, sternly:

"Delia, would it add to the welfare of the South if it should gain its independence? Would it add to *your* happiness?"

"It would," she replied. "The only respectable part of the country would then be rid of the sneaking, meddlesome North; and of course I should be happy."

"We do not see it alike," said I. "Do I understand that you wish me to become a traitor for your sake, and fight in the ranks of the rebel army, against the government of my nativity, which has never done ought but shower blessings upon me?"

"Yes!" she said, fervently, "Rebel army if you please to call it so. Listen to me, William. I am your affianced, we are plighted, and we love each other, as you say, as none ever did before. This I do not deny; but I love my country also."

"Is not this United States your country?" said I. "Then why do you wish to destroy it?"

"No," she replied scornfully. "The South is the only part of the country that deserves the name of United States. See here, I have a proposition to make you."

"Go on," said I.

"I do not believe you are a coward," she said tenderly, "but I want a proof of your devotion to me and the land I love. You can get a commission — I will see that you have one. Will you go? Here is my hand; my heart is yours, and shall go with you and be to you a talisman of safety in all danger."

"Could you marry a traitor, Delia?" I asked, for I could not get rid of that blighting idea.

"Don't call yourself that, William," she said kindly. "I am plighted to you, and as soon as you prove yourself to me and my country, we shall be one; but if not—"

"Never?" interrupted I.

"You have guessed it, William," said she. "Come, forget the harsh name of traitor, and go, will you?"

This was said with the most intense tenderness, and throwing her arms around my neck she lavished upon me a flood of kisses.

"Won't you go, dearest, for my sake?"

My mind was made up. I could not leave her, and under the impulse of her fervent kisses, forgetful of the circumstances, I replied, firmly:

"I will, Delia, and God protect me from a traitor's fate and save you from remorse if I am lost."

With the warmest protestations of love, we parted. At that moment I would have rebelled against the world for her sake. The next day I had a Lieutenant's commission, and in one month my reward came. I knew it would, for I deserved it. O, faithless woman! O more than faithless Delia! In one month she was married to another! I did not weep. I did not upbraid myself, for I then knew that she induced me to go that she might obtain that other. Remorse and despair took possession of me, and I determined to die. I sought the thickest of danger, and wantonly threw myself in the most perilous places. But fate seemed to mock me. I could not die. But to-day, thank God, fate has favored me, and death will soon blot out this enormity of my life.

That night the Lieutenant was buried, and one sad heart, at least, throbbed with pity for the erring but unhappy soldier. But what of the faithless and heartless Delia? Who shall record her heart throbs?

FRATERNIZING OF ENEMIES.

During the week of battles in front of Washington, Gen. Bayard went forward under a flag of truce to meet and confer with his old comrade in arms, the now famous J. E. B. Stuart, of the rebel cavalry.

At the opening of the war, Stuart was First Lieutenant and Bayard Second Lieutenant in the same company; but Stuart is now a Major General and Bayard a Brigadier.

During the interview, a wounded Union soldier lying near asked for water. With the familiarity of old times, Bayard, tossing his bridle to the rebel officer, said:

"Here, Jeb, hold my horse a minute, will you, till I fetch that poor fellow some water?"

Stewart took the bridle, and held the horse while Bayard went to a stream near by, and brought the wounded man some water.

6

When Stuart handed his old friend the bridle, he remarked, jok ingly :

"It is some time since I played orderly to a Union General."

"Union Generals may order you yet, Jeb," replied Bayard.

"When they find me," retorted Stewart, laughing.

The business upon which they met was soon arranged, and the old friends parted. A fight, which had ceased while they were engaged in talking, recommenced with great fury on both sides the moment each got back to his own ranks, and the two friends were again enemies

DEVOTION OF A CONTRABAND.

During the first days' fight at the bloody battle of Fair Oaks, the rebels drove General Casey's division from their camping ground, and rested for the night, confident that the morrow would give them a chance to drive the Yankee invader beyond the Chickahominy. But just at daylight that morning, Heintzelman's corps reinforced our line, and at day-break were hurled against the rebel foe For a long time the issue was doubtful. The line swayed to and fro; but at last the Excelsior Brigade — the heroes of Williamsburg — was ordered to charge. That charge is a matter of history. It gave us the battle ground of Fair Oaks.

One afternoon word was sent to General Sickles that the enemy was advancing in force, and every preparation was at once made for battle. A few shots were heard from pickets, but a few hundred yards from our battery, and then every thing was quiet. What meant that silence? What were the rebels doing? Several orderlies sent out to the pickets, failed to bring any satisfactory intelligence. General Sickles turned to Lieutenant Palmer, one of his aids, and acting Assistant Adjutant General, and directed him to take a squad of cavalry and ride cautiously out to the first bend in the road, and communicate with our pickets.

Palmer was a noble fellow—young, handsome, a perfect gentleman, a graceful rider, and a gallant soldier. He was the pride of the brigade. Forgetful of the caution given him, with the impetuosity characteristic of youth, he dashed forward at a full gallop, with saber drawn. He came to the first bend in the road, and (fatal mistake) kept on. He came to the second bend, and as he turned it, directly across the road was a company of rebel infantry, drawn up to receive him. They fired. One ball crashed through that handsome face into his brain, while another tore the arm that bore aloft his trusty blade.

The shots were heard at the battery, and in a moment Palmer's riderless horse, bleeding from a wound in the neck, galloped from the woods, followed by the squad of cavalry, who told the General of the untimely fate of his aid.

"Boys," said the General to the veterans who clustered around to hear the story, "Lieutenant Palmer's body lies in that road." Not a word more needed saying. Quickly the men fell in, and a general advance of the line was made to secure it. Whilst the cavalrymen were telling the story, a negro servant of Lieut. Palmer's was standing by. Unnoticed he left the group; down that road—the Williamsburg turnpike—he went; he passed our picket line, and alone and unattended he walked along that avenue of death to so many, not knowing what moment he would be laid low by a rebel bullet, or be a prisoner to undergo the still worse death—a life of slavery. Upon the advance of our line, that faithful servant was found by the side of his dead master; faithful in life, and faithful amid all the horrors of the battle-field ; even in death.

None but those who know the locality —the gallant men that make up Hooker's division —can appreciate the heroism that possessed that contraband. That road was lined with sharp-shooters. A wounded man once lay in it three days, neither party daring to rescue him. The act of that heroic unknown, but faithful contraband, was one of the most daring of the war, and prompted by none other than the noblest feelings known to the human breast.

TRUSTING DE LORD.

A Captain in one of the Maine regiments at Port Royal, has a colored servant named Tally, who has talked very bravely when spoken to about joining the colored brigade. To test his courage, the Captain recently told him he was about to visit the main-land, and asked Tally if he would go with him and help fight the rebels. Tally, after scratching his head and rubbing his shins a few moments, replied:

"Dun know 'bout dat, boss; I'se ober on de main a short spell ago, an' trus' de Lord ter get me ober here, an' he dun it; but it ain't best to ask too much ob de Lord. 'Spects I doesn't like to truss him agin, Boss."

A HUMILIATING MISTAKE.

Colonel Averill came upon a secesh gentleman, in Virginia, who mistook him for the renowned rebel Stewart. Eyeing him from head to foot, the rebel said:

"So you are the celebrated Stewart?"

The Colonel, who aimed to he non-committal, answered:

"It is supposed so, by *some* people."

"Well," said the man, much pleased, "Is there anything I can do for you in this neighborhood?"

"Well," said the Colonel, "I don't know. How are all the *boys*, around here?"

"Why," said the man, earnestly, "the Rangers have gone to Fredericksburg, and we don't know when they will be back; but that will make no difference to you. I will entertain you during their absence. I have been a Union man—a Minor Botts man—and have repented of that, and am now doing all I can for the Southern cause. I own thirty-five negroes, and I sent all but two to work on the fortifications at Williamsburg and Yorktown. Don't you think that will set me right with the Confederate Government? And, besides, I want to go with you to-day; I want to show you around the country."

"Well, sir," says Colonel Averill, "I think *you have* done considerable for the Confederate government, and I think it is more than likely *you will* go with me."

"I thank you, Colonel; it is an honor to go with the great Colonel Stewart, and I want you to bring all the boys to my house to-night. I have plenty of room for your whole regiment. I have bacon, flour, meal, for your men; corn for your horses; eggs in abundance, and you all shall swim in milk."

"Thank you, sir," said the Colonel, politely; "I will let you go among the boys and extend your invitation. Captain, take the gentleman among the boys."

The Captain, knowing what this meant, handed the old fellow over to the guard. When he found out that he had been trapped, he exclaimed:

"I have heard of Yankees, but this out-Yankees the Yankees! Gentlemen, what do you want with me? I am a civilian."

He afterwards found out what he was taken for.

NORTHERN BRAVERY.

Colonel Wilder's official report of the battle of Munfordsville contains the whole history of the bravery of the liberty loving heroes of the North. He says:

"If I were to give a list of those who did their whole duty, it would simply be a muster roll of all who were there; no man flinched or held back a particle."

EXPRESSIONS OF WOUNDED MEN.

It is somewhat singular that the first word that leaps to the lips of a soldier when mortally wounded, is the name of his Maker. It is an involuntary expression, prompted perhaps by the innate desire of the human soul to call upon the Supreme Power in its last moments.

"My God! I'm shot!" is the exclamation of nearly all those, especially officers, who have spoken when mortally wounded.

The following incident is an evidence of this. At one time during a battle, four out of six cannoniers, serving at one of the pieces, were wounded at the same time. A German clapped his hand to his temple, crying out:

"Mein Gott! I'm killed!"

Another placed his hand on his back, saying:

"O, Lord! I'm shot!"

Another brought his hand to his eye, exclaiming.

"Great God! I'm shot, too."

Another, who was shot in the neck, said:

"Lord! I'm burnt."

The simultaneous movement of the hands to the parts injured, and the accompanying exclamation, is remarkably singular.

PHIL. KEARNEY.

General Kearney, killed during the battles before Washington, was a remarkable man. During his residence in Paris, General Kearney was the constant companion of those officers in the French army most celebrated for valiant deeds. He delighted in the society of such as himself—soldiers in every sense of the word. He profited by their experience, discussed with them military matters, adding thus to his own acquirements the results of the study and experience of others.

Before the commencement of the present struggle, his dwelling in Paris was the rendezvous of all American officers passing through France. His hospitality was unbounded, his courtesy that of the high toned gentleman. We have seen gathered around his table there those now prominent in the rebel army—Beauregard, Lee, the Johnstons, Stonewall Jackson, Magruder, and others; and no doubt many a pang will visit their hearts when they learn that Phil. Kearney was their victim. We are assured that these rebel leaders respectfully expressed, in their letters to secessionists in Paris, their dread of the military skill and dash of "Brave Phil. Kearney," and the wonder that he was not long since appointed to some high and responsible post.

General McClellan wept when he gazed at the dead body of
the hero; and when questioned as to who should take the command of the departed, replied: "Who could replace Phil
Kearney?"

AFTER THE BATTLE.

If the battle field, in the might of its murderous rattle, is
grand and terrific, when the lull comes, when the excitement is
over, it is equally disgusting, sickening and heart-rending. Here
many of the brave soldiers lay as they had met their death. In
one part of the battle field of Antietam, in a large cornfield, just
at the edge of a wood, where the rebels appeared to have suffered
the most, their dead lay so thick that their dark forms, as an officer remarked, "lay like flies in a sugar bowl." A rifle-pit, which
was charged upon by a Pennsylvania regiment, contained heaps
of dead lying just as they had fallen—one upon the other. In
a ravine, three rebels had met their death apparently while eating their breakfast. A plate lay before them with food upon it,
containing a spoon, and around them lay the scattered fragments
of a shell which had doubtless exploded in their midst, taking
off the top of the head of one, and giving death wounds also to
the others.

It is a sorrowful sight that one sees in such a place. A hospital on the battle field comprises all that is terrible in war—
broken arms and legs, bones crushed and pulverized, flesh torn
into shreds, eyes shot out, fingers shot off—a place of groans,
of agony, of death—most merciful of deliverers—of bloody tables
and amputations, of heroic endurance, and strong natures grap-
pling with great sufferings. The surgeons and nurses worked
assiduously. Water for thirsty lips, blackened with gunpowder;
stimulants for exhausted natures; bandages and dressings for
flesh wounds; and the knife for desperate cases.

Stretched on straw, in front of a barn door, lay a Massachusetts soldier—clear complexion, glossy and luxuriant hair and
beard, a nose exquisitely chiseled, an eye black as the raven's
wing and sparkling as a carbuncle—a man that would at once
attract attention and admiration for the manly beauty of the
face and the fine proportion of the body. His brother knelt beside him, smoothing back his hair and clasping his already stiff-
ening hand. No words were spoken and no tears shed. Turning his head and fixing his gaze upon the sky, the dying soldier
lay silent, gasping, the muscles about the mouth contracted, the
nerves quivering with pain. Presently the color faded from the
lips, the face whitened till it looked as pure and clear as marble,

the eyes became dull and staring, a shudder passed through the frame, and the spirit of the patriot and christian stood revealed in the clear radiance of eternity. The agony was passed. The surviving brother, having seen the body placed in a position where he could recover it, shouldered his musket, and with heavy feet and heart, moved slowly forward to resume his place in the ranks, and his position in front of danger. This was but one of a hundred equally touching incidents. Yet there was a wonderful buoyancy of spirit among the wounded. They talked with great animation of the part they had taken in the fight of the morning, of the glorious conduct of their regiments and brigades, and made light of their wounds as an almost inevitable consequence, and from which they would speedily recover.

It is strange what a difference there is in the composition of human bodies, with reference to the rapidity with which change goes on after death. Several bodies of rebels strewed the ground on the bank, in the vicinity of the bridge. They fought behind trees, and fence-rail and stone-heap barricades, as many a bullet-mark in these defenses amply attested; but all that availed not to avert death from these poor creatures. They had become frightfully discolored in the face and much swollen: but there was one young man with his face so life-like, and even his eye so bright, it seemed almost impossible that he could be dead. It was a lovely-looking corpse. He was a young man, not twenty-five, the soft, unshaved brown beard hardly asserting yet the fullness of the owner's manhood. The features were too small, and the character of the face of too small and delicate an order to answer the requirements of masculine beauty. In death his eye was the clearest blue, and would not part with its surpassingly gentle, amiable, good, and charming expression. The face was like a piece of wax, only that it surpassed any piece of wax-work.

One other young man, beardless yet, but of a brawnier type, furnished another example of slow decomposition. His face was not quite as life-like; still one could easily fancy him alive to see him any where else than on the field of carnage; and strange, his face wore an expression of mirth, as if he had just witnessed something amusing. A painful sight especially was the body of a rebel who had evidently died of his wounds, after lingering long enough at least to apply a handkerchief to his thigh himself as a tourniquet to stop the bleeding. His comrades were obliged to leave him, and our surgeons and men had so much else to do that they could not attend to him in time. Perhaps nothing could have saved him; or perhaps, again, a skillful surgeon's hand might have restored him to life, love and usefulness. But he was doomed to lie there, sweltering in the hot sun, his throat

crisped with thirst, till the life-blood oozed away, and his weakened vitality kindly suffered him to die a pangless death.

Cool and stoical as one becomes by being continually in the
midst of such carnage, the battle-field is one of the most revolt-
ing, horrible and heart-rending sights that the wildest imagina-
tion can conjure up. In some places the dead were lying two
and three deep. The death of many is so instantaneous that
their arms are in full position of firing their pieces, while others
still retain the bitten cartridge in their mouths or hands. Here
lies one with his head buried in a mud hole, perhaps mortally
wounded, and finished by the water; there lies another like the
corpse in Peale's "Court of death," with his back across a log
and his head and feet in the water. Two others were found
clasped in each other's arms, but it was the firm grip of hate —
the clutch of death. Each had received frightful wounds, and
their sabres lay beside them, where they had probably been
thrown when the combatants grasped each other.

But all these are ever the sad results of battle. Who shall
comfort the bleeding hearts of the fathers and mothers, brothers,
sisters and wives of these wounded ones, who are, by the relent-
less hand of war, torn from their friends, and the bosoms of the
loved ones at home? There is one comfort: They gave their
lives a sacrifice to the liberty of their country. They have
fought, and bled, and died for that banner which is the only emblem of Liberty, and which, in consequence of their valor, shall
yet float in more graceful folds in the blue face of heaven, a type
to all nations of the triumph of Liberty.

A BRAVE CRIPPLE.

When the Second Vermont regiment was mustered into service,
a man named Thayer presented himself, who had a stiff wrist.
The surgeon considering the limb too much deformed, rejected
him. It seemed to be a severe blow to the young fellow, and he
actually shed tears at the refusal.

"By Gum!" he exclaimed, "I'm going to hunt them rebels in
spite of the darned old doctor. How does _he_ know what I can
do?"

"You'd better go cook, Thayer," said one.

"I'll do it, by gum!" he exclaimed; and he was as good as his
word, and when the regiment went into service, Thayer was
"slewing" the pots and kettles generally.

One day there was a battle to be fought.

"Say, Thayer," said a soldier, "can't you go out and give the
enemy a few beans?"

"Darned if I don't," said Thayer. "I'll give 'em a bean or two that I calculate they'll find pretty hard to digest."

Accordingly, when the regiment went into action, he left his pots and kettles, and taking his rifle sallied forth. At last a charge was made, and during this, the cripple found himself face to face with a rebel officer, who raised his sword and cried out: "Surrender!"

"Calculate I'd better," said Thayer, and immediately shot the officer dead.

Seeing a fine sword, sash and opera glass hanging to the rebel, he concluded to make a capture. While he was taking them off, a comrade said:

"What are you about there, Thayer?"

"Calculate this is my game, and I've a right to the feathers," he answered.

"Don't you see that you'll be surrounded in two minutes?" said his comrade, and, so saying, turned and ran. Thayer had no sooner secured the traps, than he found his comrade's caution was not exaggerated, for three or four bristling bayonets were pointing in the direction of his heart, and, before he could make up his mind what to do, four bullets burst from these muskets in the same direction; but he was not wounded. Looking around, he perceived that the field in that region was deserted, the four men and himself being the only ones near. In the distance, however, he saw a squad of his own regiment coming towards him. Immediately a Yankee trick suggested itself to him. Deliberately raising his rifle, and leveling it upon the rebels, he ordered them to stand. They, supposing the rifle was loaded, and not wishing to test his marksmanship, did as they were bid. The squad of the Second, seeing the status of affairs, hurried up, and the four rebels were captured and brought to headquarters. When he arrived at camp, Thayer found four bullet holes in his clothing. When joked about his narrow escape, he replied:

"A narrow escape's as good as a wide one, if a fellow don't get killed."

PERILS OF A SCOUT.

Among the scouts sent out during the battles on the Potomac, was Dick B., of Ohio. He had seen some perilous and thrilling adventures among the rebels, which can not be better told than in his own words.

I was out scouting, with three or four others, when we got separated, and on turning a bend in the road, I suddenly came upon a party of rebel cavalry. They commanded me to halt

I replied by firing my revolver at the foremost, and then putting spurs to my horse galloped away; but the rebels were not disposed, so easily, to lose their prey, and they followed, all of us going at a break-neck pace, and they firing upon me as they could get near enough. Presently I perceived a pathway in the woods, that led off from the main road. Into this path I turned my horse, as I thought the trees would afford me a better chance to escape them and their bullets. My horse was fleet and used to brush, and I gained on them a little. I began to think my chance was tolerable, when I came to a large tree that had blown down directly across my path, and when I attempted to leap it, my horse stumbled and fell, throwing me off, and before I could remount the rebels were upon me.

"Surrender!" shouted a sergeant, "surrender, you d—d blue-bellied Yankee, or I'll blow your heart out!"

And he pointed his revolver at me, which motion was followed by the rest of the crowd.

"See here, old covy," said I, "put up your pop-gun, and take me prisoner if you like; but don't murder a fellow in that barbarous manner."

Of course I was a prisoner, and thought it was the better part of valor to fall in and trust to chance and strategy to get me out. So I was soon in line, toted up to the rebel camp, and brought before the notorious Stonewall. The General eyed me about one minute, and then said:

"Well, sir, they tell me you are a Yankee spy."

Whew! thought I, this is more than I bargained for; but I was determined to put a jolly face on the matter, and I said:

"Yes, General, that's what they say; but you rebels are such blamed liars there's no knowing when to believe what they say. I thought the Yankees could out lie any other nation, but hang me if you fellows can't beat us."

"Ah," said the General, "You don't seem to have a very exalted opinion of your brethren."

"Why should I have?" said I. "I've lost and suffered a good deal in that same Yankee nation."

"That's strange," said the General. "Don't the Union officers treat their soldiers well?"

"They're like all other officers," said I, "good and bad among them; but that's not where the shoe-pinches. To make a long story short, although I live in Virginia, I was favorably disposed to the Union cause, but the beggarly Lincolnites wouldn't believe it; so they fed their troops on my granary and cupboard till I was about ruined, and when I wanted pay they told me I was a fool, and said if I was a good Union man, I ought to be glad to aid the Government. One day one of the officers told me if I would enlist they would think better of me, and instead of dostroying my property would protect it. So the upshot of it was, as my loyalty was doubted, I was compelled to enlist to save my property."

"That's a plausible story," said the General, "but not a very probable one. Why didn't you come into our lines at once if you wanted protection?"

"That's just what I'm coming at," said I. "I was sent out with a scouting party, and so I kept on scouting till I got within your lines and was taken by your cavalry."

"Take care, young man," said the Gederal, sternly; "I understand you attempted to escape."

This was a poser; but as I had got under way, I thought I must try and make the ripple. I felt tolerable streaked about the result, too, but I said, earnestly:

"Of course I did. Who wouldn't, with a half dozen horses and bullets after him? I hadn't time to say surrender, and besides the officer cursed me. I don't like to be cursed, it's against my principles; and then I was so mighty mad to see such beastly cowards, that I half made up my mind to get away from both sides, and go to Canada."

The General looked at me and then at his staff, and they all smiled, while I looked as sober as a deacon. I had heard that the General was a pious old fellow, and I thought this would tickle him.

"Are you willing," said he, "to take the oath of allegiance to the Southern Confederacy, and fight in our cause?"

"To be sure," said I; "I told you before that I had been trying to get into your lines. But I don't want to fight for you if I am not protected in my rights. I want my property respected."

"Where do you live?" asked he.

"At Phillippi," said I, "and I've got a nice property up there, and I want it to be taken care of."

"Well," said the General, "we're going up that way shortly, and, whether you go with us or not, we will protect your property. In the meantime I will think of your offer, but for the present, as the evidence is against you, you will be placed under guard, for you Yankees are too slippery to be trusted with too much liberty. Events show that you don't know how to use it."

After this I was kept under guard, and was treated, perhaps, as well as they were, and nothing to brag of at that. The next day there was a great battle. There was much commotion in the rebel camp; and, for fear that I should be recaptured, a guard of two was detailed to take me far back to the rear. We could distinctly hear the thundering of the cannon, and we knew that a great battle was commenced. I overheard the guard chuckling at the idea that they were exempt. This put a flea in my ear. I knew they were cowards, and I determined to manage them accordingly. My canteen had not been taken from me, and, as luck would have it, was half full of tolerable "rot gut." I also had in my pocket a large powder of morphine, which the surgeon had given me a few days before, to take occasionally: this I slipped into the canteen. After this was accomplished, I appeared to take long swigs at the canteen. At last the bait took; the boys got a smell of the whisky, and one of them, turning to me, said:

"Look here, Yankee, that whisky smells mighty good. Let us help you drink it, or you'll be so drunk, soon, that we shall have to carry you."

"All right, boys," said I, "help yourselves."

They did help themselves. The beggarly rebels soon finished the whisky, morphine and all.

"It tastes mighty bitter," said one. "What's in it?"

"Quinine," said I. "I always put quinine in my whisky this time o' year."

This satisfied them, and I soon had the satisfaction of seeing my guard tolerably drunk,—too drunk to walk, and so they tumbled down, and they did not get up again so n. Finding they were getting pretty stupid and sleepy, I shook them and said:

"See here, guard. this is a shame. How do you expect to guard me, drunk as you are?"

"Yes, guard," muttered one. "Your—turn now—you guard us. Don't leave—or—by G—d, I'll shoot you when—wake up."

"But hold on," said I! "how do you expect me to guard you when I don't know the password?"

By vigorous strokes and punches, I so far routed him that he muttered:

"Rattlesnake!"

I had no doubt but this was the magical "open sesame" that was to give me my liberty. In five minutes the men were sound asleep. The place where we were was a deep gulley in the woods, and about a mile distant was the rebel camp. My purpose was soon fixed. I swapped clothes with one, which was considerable trouble, as he was as flimsy as a rag; but I succeeded at last in making the exchange, and had the satisfaction of seeing the drunken rebel nicely buttoned up in Yankee regimentals. Taking his arms I hurried away. When I got out through the woods I came into a road, and had no sooner done so than I saw a squad of rebel soldiers.

"Halt!" was the word, which I responded to with soldierly precision.

"What are you doing here?" said the Lieutenant commanding.

I told him that two of us were guarding a prisoner, and that my comrade and the prisoner were both so dead drunk I could do nothing with them.

"That's a h—l of a story," replied the Lieutenant. "I believe you're some d—d Yankee spy. I've a mind to clip your head off, on suspicion." And he raised his sword.

"Let him prove what he says by showing us the men," suggested one of the squad.

At this they all laughed, supposing I was bluffed. But when I readily assented to this, they followed me, cautiously, however, as I suppose they feared I was leading them into ambush. When the Lieutenant saw the men—one in butternut and one in Yankee blue—as I had represented, he gave each a hearty kick and said:

"Well, this *is* a h—l of a mess. What are you going to do about it?"

"Going to hunt a wagon and have them carried on," said I.

This was satisfactory, and we parted. Finding it would not do to take the road, I skulked around in the woods all day. When night came I took as I supposed a route that would lead me to the Union camp. All night I climbed about over the hills; twice I was hailed by rebel pickets, but *rattlesnake* carried me safely by. Just at daylight I discovered a camp. I could see the tents twinkling through the strip of woods before me, and I felt certain it was the Federal camp.

When I had got about half way through the piece of woods, I saw something that completely took all the exultation of my delivery out of me. Well, I've been in many a perilous position. I have had bayonets, bullets and bowies rummaging round in the region of my loyal bosom; but never, in all my life was I so astonished and chagrined—so utterly taken down. There, in the bottom of a broad, deep ravine, not ten steps from me, lay the two drunken guards! Lord! this was a pretty fix, to be sure. I had accomplished a feat equal to the hero of Mother Goose, who went

"Fourteen miles in fifteen days,
And never looked behind him."

One of the guard was sitting up, and endeavoring to rouse the supposed prisoner; for he was still too much stupefied to recognize the cheat. Perceiving me, he sung out:

"Say, Bill, this d—d Yankee's too drunk to wake up. What's to be done with him?" Have we been here all night? Lord! what'll the old General say? Come over here."

"No," said I, feigning his comrade's voice, "We've been drunk here all night, and I'm going to report before he wakes up, or they'll have us in the guard house. You stay and watch him, while I go."

"No, let's wake the devilish lubber up, and take him where

we're going to. But blame me if I know where that is. Don't go."

"But I will," said I; and, hurrying away, I was soon out of sight. This day 1 hid myself in a hollow tree, and, when night came, 1 took a good look at the stars, and, getting my bearings, started again for the Union camp. I several times came upon the rebel pickets, but the "Rattlesnake" snaked me along without any trouble: all but one, the last one 1 came to. He was a sprightly little fellow, and appeared to be determined that 1 should go with him to headquarters. 1 offered every excuse I could think of, but it was of no avail, so I at last agreed to go, and we started. 1 went with him about half a mile, and, during this time, 1 engaged him in conversation about the affairs of the war, playing the rebel, of course, and talking in a jolly way, till, finding him a little unguarded, I sprang upon him and took him down, and, before he knew what was the matter, he was unarmed.

"Now, you beggarly whelp," said I, as I snatched his gun and sprung away from him, "about face, and put, or I'll shoot you in a minute."

The fellow was scared, sure, and lost no time in getting out of my sight. It was now beginning to grow light, and 1 found myself on the banks of the Potomac, with the Federal camp far in the distance. As there was no other mode of conveyance, I was forced to swim the river, which was no easy job, considering 1 had two muskets to carrry. However, I got safely over, and was just climbing the bank, when a musket was leveled at me, and a clear voice rung out:

"Stand! who goes there?"

This 1 knew was a Union picket; so I told him I had been taken prisoner, and had escaped; had been two days without eating; and 1 wanted him to let me go, or take me at once into camp, where 1 could get something to eat, and some dry clothes 1 had no doubt but he believed this, and would immediately comply; but the answer was an ominous click of the trigger.

"1 believe you're a real Butternut Rebel," said the picket, "and I've a notion to give you a pop, any how."

"But I ain't," said 1.

"What are you doing with them butternut regimentals on then, and them two muskets?" said he.

I saw my fix, and hungering, dripping and shivering as I was, I stood there before that grinning musket till 'I had told the whole story. Finally upon my giving him the names of our Colonel and Captain. and mentioning several other matters familiar to him, he was satisfied, for he belonged to the same regiment that I did.

LOYAL MICHAEL.

An Irishman of the 69th New York, was taken prisoner, and by some strategic movement managed to shoot his captor and escape. Taking a circuitous route, and skulking about for half a day, he came upon a group of officers. Rushing into the midst of them, and fantastically kicking up his heels in true Irish polka style, he said:

"Be Jasus, but I'm safe at last! Hurray for the Shtars and Shtripes iv me own blissid Ameriky, an' the divil flay away wid the ribbels!"

"Helloe, Paddy, what's the matter?" said one.

"Mather is it? Begorra! there'll be mather enough, out in the field yonder where I laid the dirthy spalpeen that 'ud be afther stailin' me body. Divil a won o' them's able to take the likes iv a 69th. Me name's not Paddy, at all, at all, but Michael O'Graff, jist. At yer sarvice, sir."

"You were taken prisoner by the rebels, were you?" said the officer.

"I was, si:, an' sure it's no disgrace if I get away, sir."

"And you escaped?"

"That's thrue for yer, sir.

"And you killed your captor?

"I did, yer honor, and his thavin' carkiss lies out in the field beyant, a proof iv it, sir, and an imblim iv me currige."

"You seem to be a loyal Union man," continued the officer.

"Niver a loyaller iver lammed a ribbil," answered Michael, triumphantly.

"Very good, sir." Then, turning to a subordinate, much to the astonishment of the Irishman, he continued:

"Lieutenant, secure this prisoner.".

"Holy Jasus!" exclaimed Michael; "What have I done? Begorra, thin, I'll make me word good wid ye, an' may the divil take the hindmost." So saying, and before they were aware of his object, he turned and ran with all his might; but the Lieutenant's horse could outrun him, so the loyal Michael was again a prisoner of war.

It was General Wilcox and staff whom he had encountered.

THE DRAFTED EXEMPT.

Among the able-bodied men drafted from one of the Heidelbergs, there was an obese specimen of humanity, but whom the chances hit as one of the elect. When he received his ticket, he hastened to Reading, and, knowing where lived the cutest specimen of a lawyer, he went straight to his office. Said he: " I'm drafted."

"The deuce you are; it must have been a strong man that drafted you."

" Well, I'm drafted, and I want to get out. Can't march. I'll pay well."

" Very well."

The twain proceeded to the office of the Commissioner.

"Here, Commissioner," said the lawyer, "I have got a substitute."

Commissioner looked at the wheezy specimen for some time. "He won't do; can't march."

" But he must do," blustered out the lawyer, "and you know he will do, too."

"He can't march; he *won't do*, and I can't take him."

This was what our smart friend wanted.

"He won't do, eh?"

"No, he won't."

"Well, then, scratch his name off the list; *he is drafted; and wants to be exempted.*"

The Commissioner looked at the lawyer for about a minute, then regarded the fat draft, and, without speaking a word, scratched off the name.

CHIVALRY vs. THE YANKEE.

There is considerable difference in the fighting policy of the two American armies. The contest is like that of an iceberg and a volcano: there is sizzling, smoking and gassing. Some of the fire is put out and some of the ice melted. The following joke tells the whole story:

A rebel officer once remarked that the success of the rebel army was attributable to its fiery spirit, and the violence with which it rushed into battle, and they thus beat the Yankees before they were through with their prayers.

"That is so," remarked a bystander. "You fellows threaten and then take a drink, then you brag of your chivalry and take another drink, and when you are too drunk to know any better, you rush frantically into danger. But the Yankee prays and then cleans his musket, prays again, attends to his family and prays again, and then, after this third prayer, you rebels may look out for hell.

A DETERMINED PATRIOT.

A young man with a family, a cashier in a large mercantile house in Boston, enlisted in a cavalry company. His employer did not wish to part with him, and offered to raise his wages from eight to twelve hundred dollars a year. But the soldier's reply was:

"My country needs my services, and no amount of money can change my purpose."

TURNING THE TABLES.

Major Clark Wright and his rangers were a source of great terror to the rebels of Missouri. When the war broke out he had no hesitation in expressing his sentiments; but these sentiments did not please some of the rebel brethren of the Baptist church, in that vicinity, and they accordingly determined that he should leave the country, and a committee of three was appointed to inform him of their decision. But one of them, who, although an ardent rebel, was still a friend to Wright, informed him of what was to take place. Wright and his wife then held council, the result of which was that *they would* fight.

When the committee called, they hesitated about broaching the subject, and began stammering.

"Stop!" said Wright; "I know your business, and before you tell it I wish to say a word. I have just promised my wife that I would blow hell out of the first man that told me of it, and by the Eternal God, I'll do it!"

The committee saw murder in his eye, and concluded to postpone the announcement. The next Sunday the church appointed a larger committee, it being no less than a whole company of rebels, properly officered. Wright's friend informed him of this also, and, when the day arrived when he was to be ejected from the State, Wright gave a large party and secretly sent for all his friends to come and see him. This brought 300 armed men, who promised to back him to the death. They then secreted themselves in a cornfield back of the house, and awaited their time.

After a while, eighty armed men rode up to his house, and the Captain informed Wright of their mission.

"Won't you give me two days to settle up my affairs?" asked Wright.

"Two days be d—d!" exclaimed the pompous Captain, "I'll give you just five minutes to pack up your traps and leave."

7

"But I can't get ready in five minutes," urged Wright. "I have a fine property here, a happy home, and if you drive me off I am a beggar. I have done nothing to deserve this."

"To h—l with your beggary, you must travel!" said the Captain.

"Give me two hours!"

"I'll give you just five minutes, not a second longer;" persisted the Captain. "If you ain't out in that time I'll blow your cussed abolition heart out!"

"Well, if I'must I must," said Wright manfully, and, turning towards his house as if in deep despair, gave a shrill whistle; and immediately 300 men sprang from their concealment, and surrounded the astonished Captain and his company.

"Ah! Captain," said Wright beseechingly, "won't you grant me two days — two hours — to prepare myself for beggary and starvation?".

The Captain at last found voice to say, "Don't kill me."

"Kill you!" exclaimed Wright, vehemently, "No, you black livered coward! If I want that dirty job done I'll get one of my niggers to do it. Get down from that horse!"

The result of the matter was that the whole company dismounted and laid down their arms, and then, as they filed out, were sworn to preserve their allegiance inviolate to the United States. An hour after Mr. Wright had organized a force of 240 men for the war, and by acclamation was elected Captain. The next Sunday he started with his command to join the National troops under Lyon, stopping long enough on his way to surround the Hard Shell Church, which had been the cause of his troubles. After the service was over, he administered the oath of allegiance to every one present, including the reverend Pecksniff who officiated, and then left them to plot treason and worship God in their own peculiar, pious and harmonious manner.

ADVENTURES OF A UNION PRISONER.

A prisoner, although limited in his liberties, has considerable opportunity for studying the manners and customs of the enemy.

At Baldwin we first met the motley currency of Dixie—Confederate notes, cotton bills, due bills, shinplasters, and, most curious of all, railroad money printed on second-hand paper, which had been used for ledgers and day-books. Think, ye antiquarians, of pecuniary palimpsests!

I said to the officer of the guard:

"You seem to have plenty of money hereabouts?"

"Oh, yes—all you've got to do is to print the head of a woman on a piece of brown paper, and it will pass.

We were generally respectfully treated by the rebel soldiery; the abuse we received almost invariably came from non-combatants, women, citizens, and the like. One of our party of captives—the list swelled as we proceeded—was loudly attacked with curses by a person in uniform, who rode up to him in the main street of Iuka. The Illinois officer quietly responded:

"What is your rank, sir?"

"First Lieutenant."

"In the Quartermaster's department?"

"Yes."

"I thought so."

"Why?"

"Because I have noticed, in both armies, that the men who are most malignant toward prisoners are those who never get where the bullets whistle!"

(Great discomfiture of the Quartermaster, and loud laughter and applause from the rebel soldiers who stood by.)

Next morning we were dispatched by rail to Tupelo, some twenty miles further South, on the Mobile and Ohio road. I was met at the cars by a Captain of General Moore's staff, who took me to breakfast, and played the host for the better part of the day. What a tall, round-shouldered, amiable Texan he was, to be sure! A graduate of West Point, a Secessionist from the beginning, a devotee of the doctrine of State rights and Southern wrongs, he was yet as gentle as a woman in his discourse. All that bright September morning we sat in the shade of a broad piazza—the house was deserted, as about half the houses in Dixie seem to be—and talked of history and politics. Of course we laughed at each other's "extreme views," and came to no agreement on any proposition.

"You of the North," said he, "have invaded our country."

"No, sir; Mississippi is a part of our country. Do the police of New York invade the Five Points when they go there to quell a riot?"

"You of the North have contracted an enormous debt. How are you going to pay it?"

"Fund it and pay the interest. And you of the South have a little debt of several hundred millions. How do you intend to pay that?"

"We do not intend to pay it. As soon as the war is ended we will repudiate it?"

"Will that be honest?"

"Certainly; we owe it only to our own people, and they may as well lose the principle outright as to be compelled, year after year, to pay eight per cent. interest on it."

Shade of Ricardo! there was a new idea in political economy. "But,' said I, "would not that be an outrage to the individual? Suppose your entire fortune consisted of Confederate scrip, and your neighbor's of land and negroes, would repudiation affect you both alike?"

"Oh, we'll see that each man has his proper share of Confederate scrip!"

Perhaps you will hardly believe this report of our talk; it is nevertheless true. On what a foundation of political and economical falsities is this Confederacy reared up?

That evening we left Tupelo for Jackson, by the way of the Mobile and Ohio, and Southern railroads. We saw a great deal of corn on the route and very little cotton, but the corn was not, as a rule, good. There is a large tract just before Tupelo which is a fair crop. It is said to contain 400,000 acres. If so, it would be an excellent idea for our army to move down there.

We did not see an open store between Baldwin and Jackson, a distance of more than two hundred miles. I suppose their scanty stocks of goods have been sold out and cannot be replenished.

"It looks like Sunday," said one of our party—"happy land,

> Where congregations ne'er break up,
> And Sabbaths never end."

From the moment I became an involuntary visitor in Dixie, I found myself an object of interest.

My boots were the attraction. No feat of arms, or evident superiority of mental endowment, made me the cynosure of rebel eyes.

Leather is not, in the Confederacy. The paper blockade excludes it. My boots were made by Fulton street Brooks, were of the cavalry pattern—worth, perhaps, ten dollars. Firstly, my guerrilla friends tried to steal them while I was asleep on the first night of my captivity; so says the wounded soldier who lay awake and heard them discuss the plan. At Baldwin officers and men alike worshipped those boots, and were loud in verbal adoration. At Tupelo I was offered one hundred dollars in Confederate scrip for them.

Nothing tends to raise the prices of the necessaries more than a blockade, except it be a famine, and it is even productive of that. On my journey from Tupelo to Jackson, a tall young Texan stood on the platform some thirty minutes, and gazed at me with rapt attention. Then he took courage, came in, and sat down by my side. His conversation may be condensed to this:

"Fine day. Whar are you from? You can never subjugate the South. We have plenty of arms, plenty of provisions,

plenty of everything. Good Lord! what splendid boots those
are!"

"Are boots scarce in the Confederacy?"

"I paid twenty-five dollars for those shoes." And he pointed
to a pair of flimsy pumps he wore.

"Why don't you make leather in the Confederacy?"—I said;

"Don't know how; but they are making clay pipes in Alabama."
And this was said with an air of exultation, as if to make a
red clay tobacco pipe were a triumph of mechanical art.

It seems that thus far the prosecution of the war has proved,
to the South, a bootless task. Forgive the feeble joke.

I wore during my trip an old felt hat, the ugliest on this
continent, which had been thrown aside by my Colonel. At
Tupelo I said to the genial Captain who entertained me:

"If I had foreseen this visit I would have worn some decent
head gear."

"Humph! that hat is worth thirty dollars in this town."

After this, as I gazed upon the "shocking bad hats" of these
rebel natives, I donned my dilapidated "tile" with greater satisfaction.

We reached the capital of the State about 5 o'clock Monday
afternoon. It is a decent looking town, of three or four thousand inhabitants, with that shiftless look which results from the
climate and the "institution." We were marched about the
streets for a time in a rather indefinite manner. not for show, I
fancy, but because some one had blundered. At length we were
paraded in front of headquarters, and General Tilghman, of
Fort Henry fame, stood picturesquely on the steps to receive us.
He is a well-dressed, good-looking rogue, with the smile of a
demagogue and the eye of a gamester. I use these terms ad-
visedly. The subscriber happened to be the only officer among
the prisoners, and so to the subscriber the lovely Tilghman made
this sweet speech:

"Lieutenant, you will go to Vicksburg to-morrow morning.
In the meantime you will have a private room fitted up for you,
and your meals will be sent to you from the hotel at the expense
of the Government. We desire to make you as comfortable as
possible."

We touched our Twenty-five Dollar Hat, and the crowd around
us gaped in admiration of Tilghman and that Government which,
through him, promised to pay for our supper. We lifted our
Hundred Dollar Boots with alternate step, and marched toward
the private room.

We reached the private room. It was so called because it
contained nine private soldiers. In fact, it was a guard room.
It also contained a Captain of the Twenty-seventh Illinois and
a surgeon of the Fifth Minnesota, who had come down as pris-

oners the day before   It was "fitted up" with two broken shutters and a half inch of dust lying on the floor.   The nine private soldiers, Confederate, were smoking, chewing, and playing draw poker.   The room was twelve by sixteen.

Eight o'clock came, but not the supper promised at the expense of the Government, which reminded me of the Texan Captain's repudiating policy; and also convinced me that the Confederate Government does not pay expenses.   The fact was that the keeper of the hotel received an order for it, but, like Louis Napoleon, did not recognize the Confederacy.   We rose in our wrath :

"Sergeant of the guard, your General made me some very kind promises, but they are not performed, Shoulder your musket and take me out to eat."

: He obeyed; we marched half a mile and got a supper, paying a dollar for it.   You pay one dollar per meal all over the Confederacy.   It is generally a corn meal, as it consists of corn bread, corn coffee, and corn-fed bacon.

We returned to our private room, hired a piece of blanket from the Sergeant—they have no blankets in Dixie to speak of—laid it in a corner, made a pillow of one of the broken shutters, and thereupon the Captain of the Twenty-seventh Illinois and the reliable gentleman lay down and slept the sleep of innocence.

Next morning, without breakfast, we took the 7 o'clock train for Vicksburg.   O, Tilghman!

At the depot, on his way to join Price at Iuka, we saw that chief of political sinners, John. C. Breckinridge, the man who played a game for the Presidency, got beaten, and now refuses to give up the stakes.   For this let second-rate gamblers look down on him with contempt.   He seemed to be in good health, wore a linen coat, and a sort of Bowery collar and scarf.   It was easy to detect in his manner a mind ill at ease.

To the careless observer, the South might seem a unit in its plans, both for the present and the future.   The men who talk with prisoners for the most part sing one song—

" We never will submit."

Yet underneath this external sameness lie the force of dissent and revolution.   A lieutenant of rebel cavalry at Iuka said to a friend of mine:

"I am from Memphis; owe New York City $50,000, which I am able to pay when peace comes.   I am a Secessionist from the ground up.   And I tell you, sir, we shall be successful. We will hold Virginia.   We will take Kentucky—with her consent, if we can, without it if we must.   And with our northern line on the Ohio we will build up the most magnificent aristocratic republic the world has ever seen.   D—n Democracy, we want an aristocracy—capital must own its own labor."

Yet when my friend reported this speech to another rebel officer at Vicksburg, the latter clenched his teeth and said:

"I am a 'poor white;' never owned a negro and never want to—and I can tell you that when rich slaveholders try to set up an aristocracy there will be another rebellion here on Southern soil!"

Another curious fact. On our journey from Tupelo to Vicksburg we twice drank with rebel officers this toast: "The restoration of the Union."

We were told, of course, that there were no Union men in the South. Yet two companies of Mississippians were lately recruited and drilled by our officers at Iuka, and many more individually joined Northern regiments. An Illinois Captain, who helped to drill them, told me that with two hundred cavalry at his command, he could have gone into the hill country of North Alabama and there raised a brigade of four thousand men. The prayer of Northern Alabama, as of Eastern Tennessee, has been from the beginning, "Come over and help us."

One thing I especially observed in conversation with soldiers and citizens—moderate and radical—an intense desire for peace. "When will the war end?" was the sad, weary question addressed to me a hundred times. In Vicksburg I replied solemnly:

"Well, I am no prophet, but I think that in two or three years the Union forces of the nation will fairly get under way, and begin to prosecute the war in earnest."

It was amusing to see the look of dismay which clouded the face of my inquiring enemy. No wonder they desire peace. A self-indulgent people reduced to destitution and almost total abstinence from the material comforts of life, they can not but sigh for the good old times.

The fact is, the rebellion is a gigantic game of "bluff." In cards, that is the representative game of the South, and particularly the South-West. Its greatest triumphs are achieved by betting largely, and with a confident countenance on a weak hand, and so frightening your adversary into a surrender of the stakes.

Nor is the rebel army a unit. I heard several times an expression of the opinion that half its officers ought to be shot. Bragg is especially odious. A private soldier said in my hearing:

"I reckon he'll be shot by his own men in the first fight."

About noon we rolled into Vicksburg, and were sent to the Washington Hotel, the best house in the city. There you pay $4 per day, and live on corn bread without salt in it. No milk, no tea, no coffee, no butter, no wheaten bread. We were kindly told that if we had no Confederate money, our bills would be paid by the Government. We had no Confederate money.

Next morning our deliverance came, and in company with Major Watts. the portly Confederate Commissioner for the exchange of prisoners, we boarded the steamer Paul Jones and sailed to our flag-of-truce fleet, which lay seven miles above. Its boats, eight in number, had just brought down the rebel pris-oners from Johnson's Island, Alton, Camp Douglas and Camp Butler.

As Major Watts parted from us and handed us our paroles, I said:

"Major, does this document prevent us from going up to Minnesota to fight the Indians?"

"Eh?—yes, yes, certainly."

"Are those red skins allies of the Confederacy?"

"Well—I don't know."

Nor, I fancy. do we of the North know whether or not the wrath of the Sioux is prompted by Davis, Pike & Co.

We lay alongside the steamer T. L. Magill. The blessed bun-ting of America floated brightly at the stern, a white flag waved its low wings at the bow, the gunboat Cairo gave us a grim smile with its iron lips. We stepped aboard and bade, not mournfully, good-bye to Dixie.

A REBEL OFFICER'S STORY.

At Powell's river I stopped and engaged more milk of an old Lincolnite jade, keen as a brier, and mother of three (and I don't know how many more) rather nice looking gals. She complained to me of having been rudely treated by a North Carolina officer the morning previous. Arriving at camp I informed the officer of the old lady's story, and he told me that, knowing their polit-ical status, he had placed a guard around the house, to keep any of the family from going to the Gap, while our army was cross-ing the river, and that, in the meantime, the following conver-sation took place:

Officer.—(Entering the house.) "Good morning, ma'am." No answer. "Where is your husband, ma'am?"

Old Woman.—"None of your business, you rebel you."

Officer.—"I know. He is in the Yankee army."

Old Woman.—"Well he is. What are you going to do about it? He is in the First Tennessee Federal Regiment at Cumber-land Gap, and will take off your rebel head if you go up there."

Officer.—"Yes. But we have him and your General Morgan's whole command completely surrounded—hemmed in—with an army on both sides of the Gap, and in a few days they will be starved out, and have to surrender upon our own terms."

Old Woman.—"We know all that, and are easy. But Lincoln will send an army through Kentucky, which will wipe out your General Smith, just like a dog would lick out a plate, and then you and your army of barefooted, roasting-ear stealers will have to leave here in the dark again, and badly scared at that. Besides this—"

Officer.—"That's your opinion, but you are deluded Where were you born?"

Old Woman.—"Born! Why I was born and raised in Tennessee. I am an Old Hickory Tennessean—dead out against Nullification, and its bastard offspring, Secession. But where are you from?"

Officer.—"I am from North Carolina, but a native of South Carolina."

Old Woman.—"A South Carolinian—scion of Nullification—double rebel, double devil. Old Jackson made your little turnip patch of a State walk the chalk once, and Old Abe Lincoln will give you rebels hell before spring."

Officer.—(Quitting the old lady and turning to the eldest daughter, whom he recognized as a mother.) "Madam, where is your husband?"

Young Woman.—"That is none of your business."

Officer.—"But it is my business. Where is he?"

Young Woman.—"Where I hope I'll never see him again. Where I hope you'll soon be."

Officer.—"Where is that?"

Young Woman.—"Why, a prisoner in the hands of the army at the Gap."

Officer.—"What is that for?"

Young Woman.—"For being what you are, an infernal rebel."

Officer.—"Oh, if that's all, I will send him back to you as soon as we take the Gap."

Young Woman.—"No you needn't. Cust if he ever sleeps in my bed again. Here, Bet, (calling a nurse,) take this little rebel and give him Union milk. Let us try and get the 'Secesh' out of him."

Officer.—(Turning to a Miss.) "Did you find a beau among the Yankee officers?"

Miss.—"Yes, I did; a nice, sweet, gallant fellow; one who stepped like a prince. When you become his prisoner, give him my love; and tell him for my sake to put a trace chain around your infernal neck."

Officer.—"When do you expect to see him again?'

Miss.—"Just after your General takes the next "big scare," which will be in ten days from this time."

Daylight having broken, and the army having crossed the river, the conversation I have given terminated.

FORESHADOWING OF DEATH.

Presentiments on the battle field often prove prophetic. Here is an instance: While Col. Osterhaus was gallantly attacking the center of the enemy on the second day, a sergeant of the Twelfth Missouri requested the captain of his company to send his wife's portrait, which he had taken from his bosom, to her address in St. Louis, with his dying declaration that he thought of her in his last moments.

"What is that for?" asked his captain. "you are not wounded, are you?"

"No," answered the sergeant; "but I know I shall be killed to-day. I have been in battle before, but I never felt as I do now. A moment ago, I became convinced my time had come, but how I can not tell. Will you gratify my request? Remember, I speak to you as a dying man."

"Certainly, my brave fellow; but you will live to a good old age with your wife. Do not grow melancholy over a fancy or a dream."

"You will see," was the response.

The picture changed hands. The sergeant stepped forward to the front of the column, and the lieutenant perceived him no more.

At the camp-fire that evening the officers inquired for the sergeant. He was not present. He had been killed three hours before, by a grape-shot from one of the enemy's batteries.

WIDOWS PROVIDED FOR.

When the Corn Exchange's last corps left Philadelphia, there was, among the men, one who had been recently married. While they were waiting for the order to march, the young wife was taking leave of her husband, in accents broken, and eyes that lay bedewed in tears, like violets in a summer shower. The man caressed her, but the tears still started; he told her of the patriotism and munificence of the Corn Exchange Association, yet the crystals continued to fall; he told her of the country's danger, but her anguish was not soothed. At last, weary of his endeavors, he tried another tack.

"Sally," said he, "quit crying. You see what the Corn Exchange has done. They've paid you my bounty, fitted me out, and everything."

"Yes," the girl sobbed, "but"—

"But what?"

"But if you get killed—what then?"

"Why"—the man hesitated for a moment until a lucky thought truck him—"Why then the Corn Exchange will *find you an-ther husband.*"

The ludicrousness of the idea changed the current of the girl's feelings, and a smile wreathed her pretty mouth and dimples in a manner that was pleasant to behold. The last tear rolled away, and as the word "forward" was given, she gave the young recruit a last kiss, and departed in good cheer.

A BOWIE KNIFE CONFLICT.

This rebellion has been prolific of many deeds of wanton daring, and deliberate hand to hand conflicts. The following is one of the most frightful:

A soldier belonging to the 25th Missouri and a member of a Mississippi company became separated from their commands, and found each other climbing the same fence. The Rebel had one of those long knives made of a file, which the South had so extensively paraded, but so rarely used, and the Missourian had one also, having picked it up on the field.

The Rebel challenged his enemy to a fair, open combat with the knife, intending to bully him, no doubt, and the challenge was promptly accepted. The two removed their coats, rolled up their sleeves, and began. The Mississippian had more skill, but his opponent had more strength, and consequently the latter could not strike his enemy, while he received several cuts on the head and breast. The blood began trickling rapidly down the Unionist's face, and running into his eyes, almost blinded him. The Union man became desperate, for he saw the Secessionist was unhurt. He made a feint; the Rebel leaned forward to arrest the blow, but employing too much energy, he could not recover himself at once. The Missourian saw his advantage, and knew he could not lose it. In five seconds more it would be too late. His enemy glared at him like a wild beast; was on the eve of striking him again. Another feint; another dodge on the Rebel's part, and then the heavy blade of the Missourian hurtled through the air, and fell with tremendous force upon the Mississippian's neck. The blood spurted from the throat, and the head fell over, almost entirely severed from the body. Ghastly sight, too ghastly even for the doer of the deed! He fainted at the spectacle, weakened by the loss of his own blood, and was soon after butchered by a Seminole, who saw him sink to the earth

THE HEROINE OF SPRINGFIELD.

At the time when the rebel General Price was marching his troops towards Springfield, Missouri, the report got spread about among a few loyal families that they were the Federal troops. On the strength of this news a few ventured to hang out Union flags. A rebel sergeant, noticing one of these hanging from an upper window, boldly marched in, and meeting the lady of the house, a Mrs. Hart, accosted her in the following rebellious manner:

"See here, you old she Lincolnite, just haul down that striped rag, will you?"

Now Mrs. Hart, having full confidence in the report she had just heard, looked the rude intruder full in the eye, and answered:

"No, sir; that is my flag and my window, and they are not to be parted, at present."

"The h—l you say," replied the sergeant. "Then I'll do it myself. We ain't going to have any more of them dirty rags disgracing Springfield."

Mrs. Hart sprang before him, as he stepped towards the stairs, exclaiming:

"Dare you pollute that sacred flag with your miserable rebel fingers? Shame on you! Leave my house, instantly!"

"Will you take down that flag, then?" asked the sergeant.

Mrs. Hart was alone in the house, and she felt all the peril of her situation; but she was determined to protect her flag, and she replied, firmly:

"No, sir, never! Neither shall you. Again I command you to leave my house, or you shall feel the consequence. Go about your business."

"Go about the devil!" replied the sergeant, rudely.

"There's no doubt about that," said Mrs. Hart, coolly, "and the quicker you go the better."

The sergeant was exasperated, now, and catching her rudely by the arm, he jerked her on one side, and rushed up the stairs. The brave woman followed close at his heels, and just as he had dragged the flag from the window, she caught it, and stripping it from the staff, which he held in his hand, she thrust it out of the window and held it there.

"You cussed hag!" exclaimed the sergeant furiously, "if you don't give me that flag I'll pitch you out of the window."

"Do, sir, if you dare!" said the woman. "There's a Union army coming into town, and if you don't leave you'll be made a prisoner."

"Union h—l!" said the sergeant. "It's General Price's army."

"I don't believe you, sir," replied the heroine; "but if it was the whole rebel host, this flag shall wave at the window as long as I have an arm!"

The sergeant canght her by the arm and was pulling her away from the window, when the boom of a cannon was heard.

"There," he said, "Price has come. Now you abolitionists will catch h—l!"

He had no sooner uttered this, than *crash* came a twelve pound shot through the room, not three feet from their heads, dashing the crumbling plastering in their faces.. The sergeant sprang across the room, and giving one look at the woman, rushed down the stairs; while she, the pale, but cool and fearless heroine, stood there, grand in her pallor, gloriously waving the flag from the window. When the man was gone, she fastened the flag to the staff, and replacing it in her window, started down stairs; but the excitement had been too excessive. The reaction had come, and when she reached the foot of the stairs, she fell senseless in the hall. One of her neighbors, who saw the shot pass through the house, at this moment came in to see if any one was injured, and found her in this condition. The shock had been so great upon Mrs. Hart that she lay for many weeks between life and death, but finally recovered, and still lives to see the stars and stripes floating from her window.

General Price did not bombard the city, but merely, by way of announcing his arrival, fired a twelve pounder through Main street. He took possession of the place, but did not loug retain it, for he was shortly driven out by General Curtis.

THE JOLLY SOLDIER.

It is wonderful to what an extent jollity and good nature prevails among the wounded and disabled soldiers. They seem to consider it a natural consequence of the war—a sort of matter of course affair, and bravely submit to their misfortunes with a fortitude that is truly surprising.

Among the most remarkable characters of this class, was Joe Parsons, of Baltimore, a rude, boy, who formerly belonged to that fraternity of freedom called "Roughs."

Poor Joe! his was a sad fate, though he took it pleasantly enough. He was one of the first to enlist in the 1st Maryland regiment, and marched boldly and recklessly forth at the call of his country; and all through that long, hard fought, terrific battle of Antietam. he hurled death to the foe, thinking little of himself and caring less, until an unlucky bullet passed through both his eyes, destroying his sight forever. He was taken to the

hospital, and while there he was visited by a Boston correspond-
ent, who gives the following graphic account of the interview:

Joe was busily singing "I'm a bold soldier boy." Observing
the broad bandgage over his eyes, I said to him:

"What's your name, my good fellow?"

"Joe, sir," he answered; "Joe Parsons."

"And what is the matter with you?"

"Blind, sir; blind as a bat."

"In battle?"

"Yes, at Antietam. Both eyes shot out at one clip."

"Ah, that is dreadful," said I.

"Yes, tolerable;" said Joe, "but yer see it might ha' been
worse—a heap worse. I'm glad enough that I'm alive at all."

"How did it happen?"

"Well, sir, you see I was hit, and it knocked me plum down.
I didn't mind it much. I lay there all night, and the next day
the fight begun agin, hot and heavy. The cannon boomed and
the old muskets rattled. I wanted to be with 'em—I wanted a
hand at that ar myself; but yer see I couldn't on account of my
eyes, that I hadn't got any more. I could stand the pain, yer
see, but the balls was a flying all around, and I wanted to get
away. I couldn't see nothin' though. So I waited, and listened;
and at last I heard a feller groanin' beyond me."

"Hello!" says I.

"Hello yourself," says he.

"Who be yer?" says I—"a rebel?"

"I am that," says he. "I reckon you're one of the bully
Yankees?"

"So I am," says I. "What's the matter with you?"

"My leg's smashed," says he.

"Can't yer walk?"

"No."

"Can yer see?"

"Yes."

"Well," says I, "you're a d—d rebel, but will you do me a
little favor?"

"I will ef I can."

Then I says: "Well, ole butternut, I can't see nothin'; my
eyes is knocked out; but I ken walk. Come over here. Let's
get out of this. You pint the way, and I'll tote yer off the field
on my back."

"Bully for you!" says he.

"So we managed it together. We shook hands on it. I took
a wink outen his canteen, and he got onto my shoulders. I did
the walkin' and he did the navigatin'. And ef he didn't make
me carry him to his Colonel's tent, a mile away, I'm a liar.
Hows'ever, the Colonel came up and says he:

www.ingramcontent.com/pod-product-compliance
Lightning Source LLC
Chambersburg PA
CBHW031442280326
41927CB00038B/1500